Charles J. Clarke III's

LIES and MYTHS
We have Been Taught in
SELLING NEW HOMES

HOW TO DOUBLE YOUR SALES IMMEDIATELY

| 30 SALES PRINCIPLES THAT WILL ALTER YOUR SELLING SKILLS FOREVER |

By CHARLES J. CLARKE III, MIRM

*Author of "Bulls, Owls, Lambs and Tigers® -
Personality Selling and Personality Marketing™"*

Copyright©2013 Charles J. Clarke III

All rights reserved by accordance with the U.S. copyright act of 1976. The scanning, uploading and electronic sharing, or any other sharing, of any part of this book without the permission of the author constitutes unlawful piracy and theft of the author's intellectual property. If you would like to use any portion from the book, prior written permission must be obtained by directly contacting the author and receiving written permission to do so.

Thank you for your support of the author's rights.

Library of Congress control number pending

ISBN-13: 978-1490545363, ISBN-10: 1490545360

Printed in the United States of America

"Bulls, Owls, Lambs and Tigers® is a registered Trademark of Charles J. Clarke III.

Other Trademarks of Charles J. Clarke III are:

- BOLT Selling™
- BOLT™
- Personality Selling™
- Personality Selling and Personality Marketing™
- Killer Closes™
- Killer Closes for Different Personalities™
- The Art of Asking Questions™
- Lies and Myths We Have Been Taught in Selling™
- Lies and Myths We Have Been Taught in Selling Homes™
- The Only Seven Objections in Selling™
- The Five Magic Questions™
- What Do You Think (Feel) About Going Ahead With This Today™?
- The Silver Bullet™

Disclaimer: This publication is designed to provide accurate and authoritative information in regard to the subject matter covered. It is sold with the understanding that the author is not engaged in rendering legal, accounting, or other professional services. If legal advice or other expert assistance is required, the services of a competent professional person should be sought.

-From a Declaration of Principles jointly adopted by a Committee of the American Bar Association and Committee of Publishers and Accountants.

Available through Amazon.com.

Printed by CreateSpace, a division of Amazon.com

Table of Contents

PART 1

CHAPTER	CONTENT	PAGE
CHAPTER I	INTRODUCTION AND DEFINITION OF A MASTER CLOSER	1
CHAPTER II	QUIZ TO TEST YOUR BELIEF SYSEM	5
CHAPTER III	EARNING THE RIGHT TO CLOSE MYTH #1	11
CHAPTER IV	SOCIAL FIRST MYTH #2	15
CHAPTER V	BULLS, OWLS, LAMBS AND TIGERS®	19
CHAPTER VI	SELLING THE BUILDER'S VISION MYTH #3	29
CHAPTER VII	DEMONSTRATION AS THE MOST IMPORTANT VARIABLE MYTH #4	33
CHAPTER VIII	ASKING FOR THE SALE 100% OF THE TIME MYTH #5	37
CHAPTER IX	GETTING THE CHECK THE FIRST DAY MYTH #6	47
CHAPTER X	BUYING WITHOUT THE SPOUSE BEING THERE MYTH #7	51
CHAPTER XI	CROSSED ARMS AND NO SMILE MYTH #8	55
CHAPTER XII	CONTROLLING THE SALE MYTH #9	59

Table of Contents

(CONTINUED)

PART II

CHAPTER	CONTENT	PAGE
CHAPTER XIII	STATING, RESTATING AND VERIFYING WHAT THE BUYER JUST SAID MYTH #10	65
CHAPTER XIV	AVOIDING TALKING ABOUT THE PRICE RIGHT AWAY MYTH #11	69
CHAPTER XV	WOMEN MAKING THE DECISION OF BUYING MYTH #12	73
CHAPTER XVI	CREATING URGENCY MYTH #13	77
CHAPTER XVII	MEN BEING MORE LOGICAL & WOMEN BEING MORE EMOTIONAL MYTH #14	85
CHAPTER XVIII	KITCHEN AND MASTER BATHROOM AS THE MOST IMPORTANT ROOMS MYTH #15	87
CHAPTER XIX	FINDING COMMON GROUND MYTH #16	93
CHAPTER XX	MEMORIZING SCRIPTS MYTH #17	95
CHAPTER XXI	10% CLOSING RATIO (1 IN 10) MYTH #18	101
CHAPTER XXII	NEGOTIATING MYTH #19	105
CHAPTER XXIII	FOLLOW UP AND GETTING THEM TO COME BACK MYTH #20	113

Table of Contents

(CONTINUED)

PART III

CHAPTER	CONTENT	PAGE
CHAPTER XXIV	% HAVING BEEN TO YOUR WEBSITE MYTH #21	117
CHAPTER XXV	BUYING ON EMOTION AND JUSTIFYING WITH LOGIC MYTH #22	119
CHAPTER XXVI	SELLING TO ACTIVE ADULTS MYTH #23	121
CHAPTER XXVII	SELLING RESORT COMMUNITIES MYTH #24	125
CHAPTER XXVIII	SELLING CUSTOM HOMES MYTH #25	127
CHAPTER XXIX	100+ OBJECTIONS MYTH #26	131
CHAPTER XXX	SELLING HIGH-END HOMES MYTH #27	139
CHAPTER XXXI	ASKING QUESTIONS STANDING UP MYTH #28	141
CHAPTER XXXII	BRINGING OUT THE CONTRACT AFTER THEY HAVE SAID "NO" MYTH #29	149
CHAPTER XXXIII	FLAWED PRODUCT MYTH #30	155
CHAPTER XXXIV	CONCLUSION	157
CHAPTER XXXV	SUMMARY OF "30 MYTHS" IN SELLING NEW HOMES	159

©2013 CHARLES J. CLARKE III
NO REPRODUCTION IN ANY FORM

A SPECIAL THANKS!

I WANT TO GIVE A SPECIAL <u>THANK YOU</u> TO <u>THESE</u> SPECIFIC PEOPLE THAT WERE "BEHIND THE SCENES" IN GETTING THIS BOOK TO PRESS.

THANK YOU TO:

- **C.J. CLARKE IV (CHARLES JOSEPH CLARKE IV)** - My oldest son and <u>Marketing Director</u> for Charles Clarke Consulting. He **RUNS** the company. His love, devotion and daily persistence of "Write the Books!" helped make <u>this</u> book a reality. He came up with this specific book title, "Lies and Myths We Have Been Taught in Selling New Homes™." He is also an author, actor, model and professional speaker.

- **ANNE ALEXANDER CLARKE** – <u>Editor</u> and my devoted wife. Her love, devotion, loyalty and daily persistence of "Write the <u>Books</u>" also made this book a reality. When a person hears every day, "You are Wonderful," you start believing it! Her vast business background as a Commercial Builder and Commercial Property Management Owner, contributed immensely.

- **JODI L. JENKINS** – <u>Editorial Assistant.</u> After literally 100 rewrites, Jodi Jenkins never gave up, because she wanted it to be perfect.

- **ANDREA (ANDY) CLEARY** – <u>Graphic Artist from Atlanta, GA.</u> Thanks for the cover design! andy-cleary.com

- **RUTH ANN KELLEHER** – <u>Professional Proofreader from Cedar Rapids, IA.</u>

- Besides these five, there are other family, friends, and business associates who made this book and the other books possible. They were all part of "Write the Books!" You know who you are!
Thank you!

DEDICATION

> THIS BOOK IS DEDICATED TO THE
>
> NAHB'S NATIONAL SALES AND MARKETING COUNCIL
>
> AND ALL LOCAL SALES AND MARKETING COUNCILS (PAST, PRESENT & FUTURE) AND ALL MEMBERS OF THE SALES AND MARKETING COUNCILS THROUGHOUT THE UNITED STATES
>
> *IF YOUR LOCAL BUILDERS ASSOCIATION DOES NOT HAVE A SALES AND MARKETING COUNCIL, GO AHEAD AND ESTABLISH ONE. GET HELP FROM THE NAHB'S NATIONAL SALES AND MARKETING COUNCIL.*
>
> AND TO ALL
>
> MIRMS (PAST, PRESENT AND FUTURE)

THIS BOOK IS AN ATTEMPT TO GET US ALL TO CHALLENGE AND TO CONTINUE TO CHALLENGE OUR BELIEF SYSTEMS TO MAKE OUR INDUSTRY STRONGER.

WITHOUT SALES WE REALLY DON'T HAVE AN INDUSTRY!

CHAPTER I

INTRODUCTION AND DEFINITION OF A MASTER CLOSER

THE TITLE OF THIS BOOK "LIES AND MYTHS WE HAVE BEEN TAUGHT IN SELLING NEW HOMES™" IS PRECISELY THAT. WHAT HAPPENS WITH "LIES" AND "MYTHS" IN AN INDUSTRY IS THAT THEY GET PERPETUATED FROM ONE BOOK TO THE NEXT, FROM ONE SPEAKER AT A CONVENTION TO THE NEXT AND ON AND ON. SALESPEOPLE SELL THE WAY OTHER SALESPEOPLE SELL (CC III) AND "MEDIOCRITY" GETS PASSED ON.

AN OPERATIONAL DEFINITION OF MEDIOCRITY IS APPROXIMATELY A 1 IN 20 CLOSING RATIO (AN AVERAGE/MEDIOCRE SALESPERSON)

OPERATIONAL DEFINITIONS OF CLOSING RATIOS

- **<u>MASTER CLOSER</u>** (THE BEST) 1 IN 4 TO 1 IN 5 CLOSING RATIO
- **EXCELLENT SALES PERSON** 1 IN 10
- **GOOD SALES PERSON** 1 IN 15
- **MEDIOCRE (AVERAGE) SALESPERSON** 1 IN 20
- **CLERK** 1 IN 25
- **BAD CLERK** 1 IN 30+

©2013 CHARLES J. CLARKE III
NO REPRODUCTION IN ANY FORM.

A CLOSING RATIO IS, OF COURSE, THE NUMBER OF BUYING UNITS (TRAFFIC) AS IT RELATES TO NET SALES.

DEFINITION OF A BUYING UNIT: IF THERE ARE 3 PEOPLE IN A FAMILY THAT COUNTS AS 1 BUYING UNIT.

"TRAFFIC" INCLUDES ALL TRAFFIC NOT JUST QUALIFIED TRAFFIC.

THE REASON I AM EMPHASIZING CLOSING RATIOS THIS EARLY ON, IS BECAUSE THEY ARE <u>MEASURABLE</u> AND AN INDICATION OF YOUR SUCCESS.

IF AFTER READING THIS BOOK, YOU END UP THINKING DIFFERENTLY ABOUT THE SALES PROCESS, YOU WILL ACTUALLY CHANGE YOUR BEHAVIOR AND THEN DRASTICALLY INCREASE YOUR RESULTS! YOU WILL <u>ALTER</u> YOUR CLOSING RATIO AND BE ON THE ROAD TO BECOMING A MASTER CLOSER.

THE PURPOSE OF THIS BOOK IS TO GET YOU TO THINK DIFFERENTLY ABOUT THE SALES PROCESS

This book is written in Tiger and Bull print with boxes emphasizing important points. Both Bulls and Tigers (1/2 of the population) have told us they appreciate this, because neither of them read books word for word, as Owls and Lambs do.

So, Owls and Lambs bear with us on this one. It's great information.

Also, Owls and Lambs, I realize I haven't defined my terms of Bulls, Owls, Lambs and Tigers®, but I will.

THINGS I AGREE WITH

THINGS I DISAGREE WITH

THINGS I NEED TO WORK ON

ACTION PLAN FOR ME

CHAPTER II

QUESTIONS

HELLO!

*BEFORE I BEGIN WITH GIVING YOU MY "OPINIONS" IN SELLING NEW HOMES, LET ME ASK YOU, **YOUR** OPINIONS.*

PLEASE GO AHEAD AND ANSWER THESE 30 QUESTIONS BEFORE READING AHEAD.

I'M ASKING YOU TO ACTUALLY WRITE IN YOUR BOOK, SO YOU CAN REFER BACK TO YOUR ANSWERS LATER.

*IF YOU ARE A MEGA "OWL" (VERY ANALYTICAL, NEAT AND SYSTEMS-ORIENTED) USE A PENCIL OR AT LEAST RECORD SOMEWHERE YOUR ANSWERS, FOR FUTURE REFERENCE. OWLS HAVE A HIGHER PREFERENCE FOR **NOT** WRITING IN THEIR BOOKS. LIBRARIANS TAUGHT THEM THAT AND THEY OBEYED. LAMBS (RULES ORIENTED INDIVIDUALS) ALSO PREFER NOT TO WRITE IN THEIR BOOKS.*

THANK YOU,

CHARLES J. CLARKE III

"30 STATEMENTS TO DISCOVER YOUR BELIEF STATEMENT IN SELLING NEW HOMES"

TOTAL UP YOUR TOTAL # OF YES'S AND YOUR TOTAL # OF NO'S OUT OF THESE 30 QUESTIONS.

1) A SALESPERSON HAS TO ALWAYS EARN THE RIGHT TO CLOSE. YES/NO

2) IT IS OF UTMOST IMPORTANCE TO ALWAYS TALK ABOUT SOCIAL FIRST (BUILD RAPPORT) RATHER THAN BUSINESS FIRST (COMMERCE). YES/NO

3) IN NEW HOME SALES IT IS OF UTMOST IMPORTANCE TO SELL THE CONCEPT OF THE "BUILDER'S VISION" AND TELL THE BUILDER'S STORY AT THE BEGINNING, IN THE FIRST FEW MINUTES. YES/NO

4) OF ALL THE STEPS IN THE CRITICAL PATH OF SELLING NEW HOMES, THE OUTRIGHT MOST IMPORTANT STEP IS "DEMONSTRATION," IN ORDER TO DIFFERENTIATE THE BUILDER AND THE NEW HOME FROM EXISTING (USED) HOMES AND OTHER COMPETITORS. YES/NO

5) IT WOULD BE TOO PUSHY 100% OF THE TIME, TO ASK FOR THE SALE. YES/NO

6) IT IS "VERY RARE" FOR SOMEONE TO "BUY" (GIVE A CHECK AND SIGN A CONTRACT), THE FIRST TIME THEY SEE THE COMMUNITY OR HOME IN PERSON. YES/NO

7) IF MARRIED, THEY WOULD <u>NOT</u> "BUY" IF THEIR SPOUSE IS NOT THERE. YES/NO

8) CROSSED ARMS AND NO SMILE MEANS THAT A PERSON IS DEFENSIVE. YES/NO

9) IT IS VERY IMPORTANT THAT THE SALESPERSON TAKES CONTROL AND MAINTAINS CONTROL THROUGHOUT THE SALES PROCESS, AND THAT THE BUYER IS TOTALLY MADE AWARE OF THIS. YES/NO

10) IT IS VERY IMPORTANT TO "ALWAYS STATE, RESTATE AND VERIFY" WHAT THE BUYER JUST SAID. YES/NO

11) IF A BUYER ASKS FOR THE PRICE RIGHT AWAY, THE SALESPERSON SHOULD AVOID TELLING THE BUYER THE PRICE RIGHT AWAY AND STAY ON COURSE. YES/NO

12) IF A COUPLE IS MARRIED, THE WOMAN ALWAYS MAKES THE FINAL DECISION IN BUYING. YES/NO

13) EVEN IF THERE IS NOT AN URGENT SITUATION, THE SALESPERSON NEEDS TO CREATE "URGENCY," IN ORDER TO MOTIVATE THE BUYER. YES/NO

14) MEN ARE ALWAYS MORE "LOGICAL" IN BUYING A NEW HOME, WHILE WOMEN ARE ALWAYS MORE "EMOTIONAL." YES/NO

15) THE KITCHEN AND THE MASTER BATHROOM WERE, AND STILL ARE, THE MOST IMPORTANT ROOMS IN THE NEW HOME FOR A BUYER. YES/NO

16) IT IS OF UTMOST IMPORTANCE TO FIND "COMMON GROUND" WITH THE BUYER AND MAINTAIN THAT COMMON GROUND THROUGHOUT THE SELLING PROCESS. YES/NO

17) MEMORIZING "SCRIPTS," "WORD FOR WORD," AND USING THESE MEMORIZED SCRIPTS VERBATIM IS EXTREMELY IMPORTANT FOR THE SALESPERSON TO BECOME THE ABSOLUTE BEST. YES/NO

18) A "1 IN 10" CLOSING RATIO (10%) IS THE ULTIMATE CLOSING RATIO FOR WHICH A SALESPERSON SHOULD STRIVE. YES/NO

19) IT IS BEST TO ALWAYS HAVE THE BUILDER PRICE THE HOME HIGHER THAN WHAT THE BUILDER WOULD SELL IT, SO YOU CAN NEGOTIATE THE PRICE LOWER. YES/NO

20) THE MOST IMPORTANT ACCOMPLISHMENT A NEW HOME SALES CONSULTANT CAN ACCOMPLISH ON THE FIRST VISIT, IS TO GIVE THE BEST PRESENTATION POSSIBLE TO GET THE BUYER EXCITED ENOUGH TO COME BACK.   YES/NO

21) 92% OF ALL POTENTIAL BUYERS HAVE ALREADY GONE TO YOUR WEBSITE BEFORE VISITING YOU. YES/NO

22) ALL BUYERS BUY WITH EMOTION AND JUSTIFY IT WITH LOGIC. YES/NO

23) IN SELLING TO ACTIVE ADULT BUYERS (50 YEARS+) THEY REALLY NEED TO BE TREATED DIFFERENTLY AND CERTAINLY WOULD NOT BUY ON THE FIRST DAY. YES/NO

24) SELLING RESORT COMMUNITIES IS VERY DIFFERENT FROM SELLING NON-RESORT COMMUNITIES. YES/NO

25) SELLING CUSTOM HOMES "ON THEIR LOT" IS VERY DIFFERENT, AND IF POTENTIAL BUYERS DON'T ALREADY HAVE THEIR OWN LOT (LAND) IN PLACE, THEY CERTAINLY WOULD NOT PURCHASE ON THE FIRST DAY. YES/NO

26) THERE COULD BE LITERALLY 100+ OBJECTIONS OF WHY A BUYER DOESN'T BUY ONE OF MY HOMES. YES/NO

27) SELLING HIGH END HOMES REQUIRES A VERY DIFFERENT SKILL SET THAN SELLING ENTRY-LEVEL HOMES. YES/NO

28) IT IS BEST TO ALWAYS ASK QUALIFYING QUESTIONS (READY, WILLING, & ABLE), STANDING UP OVER THE COMMUNITY MAP WHERE THE BUYER IS RELAXED, RATHER THAN GOING INTO YOUR OFFICE IN THE FIRST COUPLE OF MINUTES. YES/NO

29) EVEN IF THE BUYER IS A READY, WILLING, AND ABLE BUYER AND SAYS "NO, THEY DO NOT WANT TO GO AHEAD WITH THIS TODAY," IT WOULD BE RUDE AND PUSHY TO BRING OUT THE PURCHASE AGREEMENT AND START WRITING ON IT. YES/NO

30) MASTER CLOSERS CANNOT OVERCOME BAD OR FLAWED DESIGN AND PRODUCT. YES/NO

TOTAL # OF YES'S_____   TOTAL # OF NO'S_____

PLEASE DO THIS TEST AND TOTAL YOUR ANSWERS BEFORE YOU READ ON!

WHEN I DO THIS AND WHEN MASTER CLOSERS DO THIS, WE END UP WITH **ZERO** YES'S. THE AVERAGE NUMBER OF YES'S WE FIND ARE ABOUT 50% OR HIGHER AND THERE ARE ALWAYS SOME THAT HAVE ALL YES'S.

AGAIN, THERE ARE NOT NECESSARILY RIGHT OR WRONG ANSWERS. IT'S JUST YOUR OPINION. HOWEVER, WOULD YOU AGREE THAT YOUR "OPINIONS" ACTUALLY SHAPE YOUR PERFORMANCE IN SELLING?

THE MORE YES'S YOU HAVE THE MORE "BLOCKS" YOU HAVE.

THERE IS A DIRECT CORRELATION BETWEEN "ZERO YES'S" AND BEING A MASTER CLOSER.

IF YOU HAVE 30 NO'S AND ZERO YES'S, "DEMAND YOUR MONEY BACK," BECAUSE YOU ARE "ALREADY THERE!"

THINGS I AGREE WITH

THINGS I DISAGREE WITH

THINGS I NEED TO WORK ON

ACTION PLAN FOR ME

CHAPTER III

LET'S LOOK AT THE FIRST QUESTION AND SEE HOW OUR OPINIONS COULD AFFECT OUR CLOSING RATIO AND PERFORMANCE.

THEN BEFORE WE EXAMINE THE OTHER QUESTIONS FROM 2 TO 30 WE WILL TAKE A LOOK AT MY LIFELONG WORK OF "BULLS, OWLS, LAMBS AND TIGERS®: PERSONALITY SELLING™" TO SEE WHY THE REST OF MY ANSWERS ARE ALWAYS NO.

> **QUESTION #1:** DOES A SALESPERSON HAVE TO ALWAYS EARN THE RIGHT TO CLOSE? YES/NO

LIE/MYTH #1: WE NEED TO EARN THE RIGHT TO CLOSE.

IF YOU PUT "YES," LOOK AT THE RESTRICTIONS YOU PUT ON YOURSELF. YES, I KNOW ALMOST EVERY BOOK ON THIS SUBJECT OF CLOSING AND EVERY SPEAKER SAYS THAT YOU HAVE TO "EARN THE RIGHT TO CLOSE" (ONE OF THE FIRST LIES WE HAVE BEEN TAUGHT), BUT ISN'T THAT "SUBJECTIVE?" WHAT DOES IT MEAN TO "EARN THE RIGHT?"

THIS IS MY BELIEF AND THE BELIEF OF MOST "MASTER CLOSERS" (1 IN 5 CLOSING RATIO).

A SALESPERSON IN NEW HOME SALES HAS "EARNED THE RIGHT TO CLOSE" IF THE BUYER WALKS INTO THEIR MODEL OR THEIR PLACE OF BUSINESS.

LOOK AT THE DIFFERENCE BETWEEN THESE 2 OPINIONS:

1) HAVING TO EARN THE RIGHT TO CLOSE, OR
2) CLOSING EVERYONE, NO MATTER IF YOU HAVE EARNED THE RIGHT TO DO SO OR NOT.

MY OPINION AND THE OPINION OF MASTER CLOSERS IS:

> # "CLOSE EVERYONE," WHETHER YOU HAVE "EARNED" IT OR NOT

WHERE DID THIS SILLY NOTION OF HAVING TO EARN THE RIGHT TO CLOSE IN OUR INDUSTRY COME FROM?

THE OPINION OF THIS BOOK IS:

"CLOSING IS THE MOST IMPORTANT PART OF THE SELLING PROCESS," MORE IMPORTANT THAN ANY OTHER ASPECT, WITH ONE "CAVEAT,"

> # CLOSE ACCORDING TO "THEIR" PERSONALITY, BUT CLOSE EVERYONE!

"IT'S ALL IN THE PRESENTATION – YOU WON'T OFFEND ANYONE."

JUMPING AHEAD, I AM RECOMMENDING THAT YOU 100% OF THE TIME, ALL THE TIME WITH EVERYONE, ALWAYS, NO EXCEPTIONS, ASK EVERYONE "WHAT DO YOU THINK (OR FEEL) ABOUT GOING AHEAD WITH THIS TODAY™?

"THINK" IS FOR BULLS AND OWLS.	"FEEL" IS FOR LAMBS AND TIGERS

THE OPPOSITE OF THIS WOULD BE TO BE "SUBJECTIVE" AND FOR <u>YOU</u> TO <u>DECIDE</u> AND CONTEMPLATE IF YOU HAD EARNED THE RIGHT TO CLOSE.

<u>YOUR SUBJECTIVE</u> OPINION COULD BE:

- DID I DO THE ENTIRE CRITICAL PATH?
- DID I GIVE THEM ALL THE INFORMATION THEY NEEDED?
- WERE THEY A "BE BACK" OR WAS IT THEIR FIRST TIME IN?
- WERE THEY QUALIFIED?

MORE ON THAT LATER, BUT FOR NOW I BELIEVE (KNOW) IT IS A <u>MYTH</u> THAT WE NEED TO EARN THE RIGHT TO CLOSE.

> **I WOULD "RATHER" EARN THE RIGHT TO CLOSE AND DO ALL THE STEPS OF THE CRITICAL PATH OF SELLING, BUT IF I DON'T, I'M CLOSING ANYWAY.**
>
> **CHARLES J. CLARKE III**

IF YOU HAD PUT "YES" TO THIS, HAVE I DONE ANYTHING TO CHANGE YOUR OPINION TO "NO?"

THINGS I AGREE WITH

THINGS I DISAGREE WITH

THINGS I NEED TO WORK ON

ACTION PLAN FOR ME

CHAPTER IV

> **QUESTION #2:** IT IS OF UTMOST IMPORTANCE TO ALWAYS TALK ABOUT SOCIAL FIRST (BUILD RAPPORT) RATHER THAN BUSINESS (COMMERCE) FIRST.

LIE/MYTH #2: IT IS OF UTMOST IMPORTANCE TO TALK ABOUT SOCIAL FIRST THEN POSSIBLE BUSINESS LATER.

THIS AND MANY OF THE FOLLOWING QUESTIONS HAVE TO DO WITH MY "BULLS, OWLS, LAMBS AND TIGERS®: PERSONALITY SELLING™."

BULLS AND OWLS, MY TWO ANIMALS THAT ARE LESS SOCIAL AND SHOW LESS EMOTION, TELL US THAT THEY REALLY DO NOT WANT SOCIAL FIRST. THEY BOTH WANT BUSINESS FIRST AND THEY ACCOUNT FOR APPROXIMATELY 50% OF THE POPULATION.

A GOOD MIND SET IS APPROXIMATELY 25% OF THE POPULATION IS REPRESENTED BY EACH ANIMAL PERSONALITY. ASK AROUND! ASK OTHERS! LOOK AT YOUR OWN EXPERIENCES! THIS IS BASED ON OUR HARD CORE SCIENTIFIC RESEARCH.

AGAIN, MANY BOOKS AND SPEAKERS SAY "BUILD RAPPORT," GET TO KNOW THE BUYER FIRST, OFFER EVERYONE WATER OR COFFEE. YES, IT'S GOOD TO "OFFER" EVERYONE THAT, BUT BULLS AND OWLS HAVE A HIGHER PROBABILITY OF SAYING "NO" BECAUSE THEY JUST WANT BUSINESS FIRST AND SOCIAL LATER (IF AT ALL).

SALESPERSON SAYS, "I JUST MADE A FRESH POT OF COFFEE. WOULD YOU LIKE SOME?"

THE BULLS SAYS "NO."

THE SALESPERSON SAYS, "OH, COME ON, DON'T YOU LIKE COFFEE?"

THE POTENTIAL BULL BUYER ACTUALLY STARTS TO GET IRRITATED AND ASKS "WHAT'S THE PRICE OF THIS HOME?"

DO YOU, AS THE READER, AGREE OR DISAGREE WITH WHAT I'M SAYING?

I'M SUGGESTING THAT APPROXIMATELY 50% OF ALL POTENTIAL BUYERS ARE BULLS AND OWLS AND WANT BUSINESS FIRST RATHER THAN SOCIAL FIRST.

IF YOU ARE FAMILIAR WITH MY "BULLS, OWLS, LAMBS AND TIGERS®" OR ARE FAMILIAR WITH OTHER PERSONALITY TYPOLOGIES, THEN YOU KNOW WHAT I AM SAYING IS "SPOT ON" TRUE.

PLEASE ALLOW ME TO DIGRESS FROM THE QUESTIONS AND GIVE YOU A BRIEF SYNOPSIS OF MY "BOLT™" SYSTEM.

OWLS WILL DISLIKE THIS A LOT, BECAUSE THEY WOULD RATHER GO IN SEQUENCE AND COVER ALL THE QUESTIONS FIRST, BEFORE ANALYZING THE ANIMAL PERSONALITIES. TRUST ME! "A JEDI I AM." I KNOW WHAT I'M DOING, AFTER 30+ YEARS OF CONSULTING TO THE BUILDING INDUSTRY AND GIVING SEMINARS TO CREATE MASTER CLOSERS.

ASK 10 PEOPLE AT RANDOM, OR EVEN IN YOUR OWN COMPANY, AND YOU WILL FIND APPROXIMATELY HALF WILL SAY THEY DON'T WANT SOCIAL FIRST.

YOUR THOUGHTS?

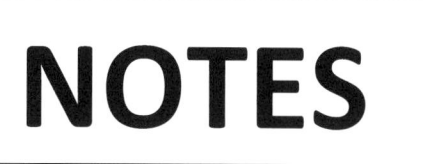

THINGS I AGREE WITH

THINGS I DISAGREE WITH

THINGS I NEED TO WORK ON

ACTION PLAN FOR ME

CHAPTER V

This chapter is an excerpt from Charles J. Clarke III's "Bulls, Owls, Lambs and Tigers®: Personality Selling™."

BULLS, OWLS, LAMBS AND TIGERS®

READ EACH DESCRIPTION AND THEN RANK IN ORDER WHICH ONE IS MOST LIKELY YOU (2ND, 3RD, 4TH). ACTUALLY WRITE IT DOWN.

THE BULL (CONTROL) #_____

- BOTTOM LINE, GET TO THE POINT
- CAN BE SOMEWHAT ABRASIVE PERSONALITY

THE OWL (ORDER) #_____

- EXTREMELY ANALYTICAL. DETAIL ORIENTED
- PERSON WHO WANTS TO CORRECT EVERYTHING YOU DO

THE LAMB (PLEASING OTHERS) #_____

- PERSON WHO WANTS TO PLEASE EVERYBODY
- TAKES A LONG TIME TO MAKE UP THEIR MIND

THE TIGER (FUN AND EXCITEMENT) #_____

- FUN AND EXCITING TYPE OF PERSON
- DISTRACTED BY SHINY OBJECTS, WITH LOW ATTENTION SPAN

I AM A _____ WITH _____.

BULLS, OWLS, LAMBS AND TIGERS® IS NOT GENDER BASED

½ THE BULLS ARE WOMEN AND ½ THE LAMBS ARE MEN. IT IS NOT GENDER BASED.

YES I DO KNOW MY BIOLOGY, BUT IN MY ANIMAL PERSONALITY SYSTEM, ½ THE BULLS ARE WOMEN

"IF A SALESPERSON ALWAYS SELLS THE WAY THEY WOULD LIKE TO BE SOLD, THEY COULD BE LOSING APPROXIMATELY ½ TO ¾'S OF THEIR POTENTIAL SALES."

CHARLES J. CLARKE III

"IF A MARKETING PERSON ALWAYS MARKETS THE WAY THEY WOULD LIKE TO BE MARKETED TO, THEY WILL **NOT** BE REACHING ABOUT ½ TO ¾'S OF THEIR POTENTIAL MARKET."

CHARLES J. CLARKE III

> "IF A BUILDER ALWAYS BUILDS WHAT THEY LIKE AND PUTS IN THE FEATURES THEY LIKE, THEY WILL NOT BE REACHING 50% TO 75% OF THEIR POTENTIAL CUSTOMERS."
>
> CHARLES J. CLARKE III

THINK ABOUT THOSE THREE STATEMENTS. WHAT DO YOU THINK?

LET'S GO BACK TO YOUR ANSWERS ON WHERE YOU THINK YOUR ANIMAL PERSONALITY IS.

AN ANSWER I GET FROM SOME PEOPLE IN MY SEMINARS IS "WELL I THINK I HAVE ALL FOUR OF THESE CHARACTERISTICS IN ME." WHAT A COP OUT! (THAT'S A BULL PHRASE.)

OF COURSE WE ALL HAVE ALL FOUR OF THESE ANIMALS IN US, BUT EVERYONE HAS ONE THAT IS THE MOST "DOMINANT" AND ONE THAT IS THE LEAST.

"OK," SOME PEOPLE ARE "CLOSE" ON SOME OF THEM, BUT YOU KNOW WHICH ONE IS MOST LIKE YOU AND LEAST LIKE YOU.

ACTUALLY IN THIS FIRST PASS AT JUDGING OUR OWN PERSONALITY, ABOUT HALF THE PEOPLE REALLY DON'T SEE THEMSELVES AS THEY REALLY ARE.

IT'S IN OUR DNA!

WE ARE BORN WITH THIS PERSONALITY JUST LIKE WE ARE BORN WITH BLUE OR BROWN EYES.

WHEN I WAS GETTING MY ADVANCED DEGREES IN THE BEHAVIORAL SCIENCES, THE MAIN PREMISE AT THAT TIME WAS OUR PERSONALITY COMES FROM OUR ENVIRONMENT. NOW, SOCIOLOGISTS AND PSYCHOLOGISTS LEAN TOWARD THE IDEA THAT IT'S MORE BASED ON HEREDITY. IT'S THE OLD NATURE VS NURTURE ARGUMENT (HEREDITY=NATURE, ENVIRONMENT=NURTURE) I BELIEVE IT IS BOTH, AND MY PREMISE IS MOST PEOPLE REALLY DON'T CHANGE THEIR PERSONALITY.

MY POINT IS IT HAS BEEN PROVEN THAT DIFFERENT PEOPLE THINK IN DIFFERENT WAYS. THEY SORT DATA DIFFERENTLY AND SOMETIMES COME TO DIFFERENT CONCLUSIONS AND HAVE DIFFERENT RESULTS. I'M SURE YOU AGREE WITH THIS, DON'T YOU?

DO PEOPLE CHANGE? CAN THEY CHANGE THEIR PERSONALITY? MY ANSWER IS THEY CAN "MODIFY" AND "ADAPT" BUT NOT REALLY CHANGE.

WHAT DO YOU THINK?

THIS IS JUST A THUMB NAIL SKETCH OF EACH ANIMAL. AGAIN, PLEASE REFER TO MY FULL VOLUME BOOK, "BULLS, OWLS, LAMBS & TIGERS® PERSONALITY SELLING™ AND PERSONALITY MARKETING™."

OTHER QUICK POINTERS ABOUT OUR 30+ YEAR RESEARCH ON EACH ANIMAL PERSONALITY:

BULLS AND TIGERS (COMBINED ARE APPROXIMATELY 50% OF THE POPULATION) SAY THEY:

1) HAVE BOUGHT A HOME THE FIRST DAY
2) WOULD BUY A HOME THE FIRST DAY IF THEY WERE READY, WILLING AND ABLE
3) SAY THEY WOULD PREFER TO BUY THE FIRST DAY

IF YOU ARE AN OWL OR LAMB, YOU JUST DO **NOT** BELIEVE THAT LAST STATEMENT. WHY? BECAUSE **YOU** WOULD NOT DO THAT **YOURSELF**!

WE JUDGE OTHER PEOPLE OUT OF OUR OWN BEHAVIOR AND THUS LOSE POTENTIAL SALES.

YOUR THOUGHTS?

IF YOU WANT TO TAKE A QUICK PERSONALITY TEST "ONLINE" FOR $10, GO TO PersonalitySellingHomes.com. IT WILL NOT ONLY TELL YOU YOUR PERSONALITY, BUT IT WILL GIVE YOU WHAT YOU PERSONALLY WANT IN A HOME, ETC.

BRIEF SUMMARY OF MY FOUR ANIMALS

THE BULL

- LIKES THE BOTTOM LINE – "GET TO THE POINT" (NOT A TO Z, JUST Z) (THEY ASK ABOUT PRICE RIGHT AWAY)
- FAST TO DECIDE (THEY SAY THEY HAVE BOUGHT THE FIRST DAY AND WOULD PREFER TO BUY THE FIRST DAY)
- FAST-PACED
- YOU BUILD RAPPORT WITH THEM BY NOT EMPHAZING SOCIAL FIRST
- RESULTS ORIENTED
- NEEDS TO CONTROL SITUATION
- PRESTIGE AND STATUS ARE MORE IMPORTANT THAN SECURITY
- LIKES CHALLENGES
- LIKES FREEDOM FROM CONTROL
- BUSINESS FIRST, THEN POSSIBLE SOCIAL (THEY WANT COMMERCE FIRST)
- LOVES TO NEGOTIATE – (THEY BUY WHEN THEY BELIEVE NO ONE ELSE WILL GET A BETTER PRICE) YOU DO NOT HAVE TO LOWER THE PRICE WITH THEM. THEY JUST NEED TO KNOW NO ONE IS GOING TO GET A BETTER PRICE.

FOLLOW-UP FOR THE BULL

- GIVE THEM A REASON TO BUY NOW. (URGENCY CLOSES WORK WELL WITH BULLS) CAPABLE OF FAST DECISION MAKING.
- ALWAYS HAVE SOMETHING FOR THEM WHEN YOU PHONE OR WRITE. BULLS DO NOT WANT A SOCIAL CALL AND THEY WILL EXPECT YOU TO GET TO THE POINT OR THE REASON FOR THE CALL.
- BUSINESS FIRST AND THEN SOCIAL POSSIBLY NEXT.

- WANTS TO KNOW HOW THIS PRODUCT WILL HELP OR AFFECT THEM ONLY. EVEN A BULL WITH LAMB

TENDENCIES WANTS TO KNOW THE "ME" RESULTS FIRST AND THEN HOW IT WILL AFFECT OTHERS.

➤ LOVES TO NEGOTIATE AND HAS TO FEEL THAT THEY RECEIVED A "ONE OF A KIND" PRODUCT, PRICE OR "DEAL." THEY BUY BECAUSE THEY LIKE IT, NOT BECAUSE YOU BUILD VALUE.

➤ FREQUENCY OF FOLLOW-UP SHOULD BE LIMITED AS WELL AS CONTENT. STATE YOUR PURPOSE FOR WRITING OR CALLING IN YOUR FIRST REMARKS. SINCE BULLS WILL BUY THE FIRST DAY, FOLLOW-UP IS USUALLY AFTER THE SALE.

©2013 CHARLES J. CLARKE III

BULLS, OWLS, LAMBS AND TIGERS® IS A REGISTERED TRADEMARK OF CHARLES J. CLARKE III
ALL RIGHTS RESERVED. NO REPRODUCTION IN ANY FORM.

THE OWL

- LIKES DETAIL AND FULL PRESENTATION FROM A TO Z (THEY ASK MORE QUESTIONS THAN ANY OF THE OTHER ANIMALS.)
- TAKES TIME TO DECIDE AND IS SLOW PACED
- VERY TIME CONSCIOUS AND EARLY FOR APPOINTMENTS
- NO MISTAKES (YOURS OR THEIRS)
- DOES NOT LIKE OVER-EXCITEMENT AND EMOTIONALISM
- SECURITY MORE IMPORTANT THAN PRESTIGE AND STATUS
- LIKES BEING ALONE, SOLITUDE
- BUSINESS FIRST, THEN SOCIAL (THEY REALLY DON'T WANT TO DRINK YOUR COFFEE)
- THEY "BUY" WHEN ALL THEIR QUESTIONS HAVE BEEN ANSWERED, AND THEY HAVE **LOTS** OF QUESTIONS

FOLLOW-UP FOR THE OWL

- AFTER A VERY DETAILED PRESENTATION FROM "A TO Z," AN OWL CAN BE SOLD ON THE SPOT IF THEY HAVE BEEN LOOKING FOR SOME TIME. IF THERE ARE ANY DETAILS MISSING THEY WILL NEED TO BE ADDRESSED SYSTEMATICALLY IN YOUR FOLLOW-UP. ALSO NOTE THAT OWLS HAVE ALREADY VISITED YOU ON THE WEBSITE
- AN OWL WILL BE EARLY FOR FOLLOW-UP APPOINTMENTS
- STICK TO BUSINESS AND COVER ANY MISTAKES
- MAKE DOUBLY SURE THAT YOU "DOT YOUR I'S AND CROSS YOUR T'S"
- KEEP THINGS NON-EMOTIONAL. EXPLORE THE PRACTICAL REASONS TO BUY THE PRODUCT
- OWLS BUY WITH LOGIC AND JUSTIFY WITH LOGIC (THEY DO NOT BUY ON EMOTION)
- THEY DO NOT LIKE URGENCY CLOSES OR TAKE AWAY CLOSES. THEY RESPOND NEGATIVELY TO BOTH

©2013 CHARLES J. CLARKE III

BULLS, OWLS, LAMBS AND TIGERS® IS A REGISTERED TRADEMARK OF CHARLES J. CLARKE III ALL RIGHTS RESERVED. NO REPRODUCTION IN ANY FORM.

THE LAMB

- BE THEIR FRIEND, GIVE DIRECTION, AND SHOW SUPPORT
- SLOW TO DECIDE AND OFTEN CHANGE THEIR MINDS (HIGH BUYER'S REMORSE)
- UNDERSTANDS YOUR MISTAKES AND FEELS BAD ABOUT THEIR MISTAKES
- VERY EMOTIONAL
- SECURITY IS MORE IMPORTANT THAN PRESTIGE AND STATUS
- AVOIDS CONFLICT
- WANTS PROTECTION AND PEACE
- SOCIAL FIRST THEN BUSINESS, NEED TO BUILD RAPPORT

FOLLOW-UP FOR THE LAMB

- ABOVE ALL, BE THEIR FRIEND, GIVE DIRECTION AND SHOW SUPPORT.
- LAMBS ARE VERY CONCERNED ABOUT HOW THEIR PURCHASE WILL AFFECT OTHERS.
- TALK EMOTIONALLY ABOUT HOW MUCH THEIR FAMILY AND FRIENDS WILL ENJOY THEIR NEW HOME.
- THEY WILL NEED TO BE REASSURED OVER AND OVER AGAIN ABOUT WARRANTY AND ON-SITE SERVICE DEPARTMENT, SHOULD ANYTHING GO WRONG.
- SECURITY OF THE PURCHASE IS EXTREMELY IMPORTANT TO THEM.
- THEY WANT TO KNOW THAT THERE HAVE BEEN MANY SATISFIED CUSTOMERS BEFORE THEM; NOT JUST OF THIS COMPANY, BUT ALSO OF THIS PRODUCT. (TESTIMONIALS VERY IMPORTANT.)
- AVOID PRESSURE SALES. INSTEAD, BE THEIR FRIEND AND DIRECT THEM TOWARD A DECISION AND HELP THEM MAKE THAT DECISION. EVENTUALLY <u>TELL</u> THEM TO BUY IN A SOFT WAY.
- THEY DO NOT LIKE URGENCY CLOSES AND RESPOND NEGATIVELY TO "URGENCY CLOSES" OR "TAKE AWAY CLOSES."
-

©2013 CHARLES J. CLARKE III

THE TIGER

- NOT INTO DETAILS – PREFERS OTHERS TO TAKE CARE OF THE DETAILS
- FAST TO DECIDE AND WILL BUY THE FIRST DAY
- FAST-PACED AND IS OFTEN LATE FOR APPOINTMENTS
- LOVES RECOGNITION AND EMOTION. LIKES EXCITEMENT
- PRESTIGE AND STATUS ARE MORE IMPORTANT THAN SECURITY
- LIKES A CHALLENGE
- SOCIAL RELATIONSHIPS ARE IMPORTANT
- SOCIAL FIRST, THEN BUSINESS

FOLLOW-UP FOR THE TIGER

- A TIGER WANTS SOCIAL, THEN BUSINESS. AFTER YOUR FIRST ENCOUNTER, MAKE SOME NOTES ABOUT WHAT FAVORITE TEAMS OR ACTIVITIES AND VACATIONS THEY HAVE PLANNED AND REFER TO ANY CURRENT NEWS OR RECENT WINS IN YOUR FOLLOW-UP. IF IT IS A TIGER WITH LAMB TENDENCIES, ASK ABOUT THEIR FAMILY.
- THEY ARE FAST DECISION-MAKERS AND BUY WHEN THEY ARE EXCITED ABOUT THE PRODUCT.
- GET THEM EXCITED AND CLOSE THE SALE THE FIRST DAY.
- THE ATTENTION SPAN OF A TIGER IS SHORT.
- IF YOU DON'T CLOSE A TIGER THE FIRST DAY YOU PROBABLY WON'T SEE THEM AGAIN.
- TIGERS ENJOY THE LIMELIGHT AND RECOGNITION. REMIND THEM HOW GREAT THEIR FRIENDS WILL THINK THEY ARE BECAUSE OF THEIR NEW HOME.
- KEEP THE FOLLOW-UP EXCITING, TO THE POINT, VISUAL, SOCIAL FIRST, NOT MUCH DETAIL, VARIED AND TAILOR-MADE.

©2013 CHARLES J. CLARKE III

BULLS, OWLS, LAMBS AND TIGERS® IS A REGISTERED TRADEMARK OF CHARLES J. CLARKE III
ALL RIGHTS RESERVED. NO REPRODUCTION IN ANY FORM.

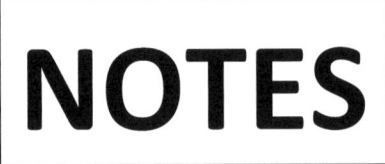

THINGS I AGREE WITH

THINGS I DISAGREE WITH

THINGS I NEED TO WORK ON

ACTION PLAN FOR ME

CHAPTER VI

> **QUESTION #3:** IN NEW HOMES SALES IT IS OF UTMOST IMPORTANCE TO SELL THE CONCEPT OF THE "BUILDER'S VISION" AND TELL THE BUILDER'S STORY AT THE BEGINNING, IN THE FIRST FEW MINUTES. YES/NO

LIE/MYTH #3: IT IS OF UTMOST IMPORTANCE TO SELL THE CONCEPT OF THE "BUILDER'S VISION" AT THE VERY BEGINNING.

MOST EVERY PUBLIC BUILDER AND OTHER LARGE INDEPENDENT BUILDERS WILL PROBABLY CRINGE AT THIS "MYTH", BECAUSE THEY ALL INSIST THAT THIS HAS TO BE DONE TO SEPARATE THEM FROM THE COMPETITORS IN THE VERY BEGINNING.

I'M NOT SAYING THIS ISN'T IMPORTANT. I'M JUST SAYING THAT "TIMING IS EVERYTHING!"

ASK YOURSELF, ASK OTHERS, IF YOU OR OTHERS WOULD CARE ABOUT, OR WANT TO KNOW ABOUT THE BUILDER'S STORY AND THE BUILDER IN THE FIRST THREE MINUTES (OR AT ALL.)

- BULLS TELL US "NO"
- TIGERS TELL US THEY WOULDN'T BE PAYING ATTENTION
- LAMBS WOULD BE POLITE AND LISTEN, BUT WOULD RATHER NOT HEAR ABOUT IT IN THE BEGINNING
- OWLS DO CARE

SO APPROXIMATELY 75% OF POTENTIAL BUYERS CONSISTENTLY TELL US THEY DO NOT WANT TO HEAR THE "BUILDER'S STORY" IN THE BEGINNING, SOME EVENTUALLY (AND SOME NOT AT ALL).

OWLS HAVE ALREADY READ AND RE-READ ON THE WEB SITE THIS INFORMATION.

I HAVE COPIES OF THE SALES TRAINING MANUALS OF MOST ALL OF THE PUBLIC BUILDERS AND LARGE INDEPENDENT NATIONAL BUILDERS AND MOST ALL OF THEM STRESS HOW IMPORTANT THIS IS. OF COURSE THEY DO! THEY ALMOST HAVE TO! YET AGAIN, TIMING IS EVERYTHING!

HOWEVER, THE TRUTH IS, IT IS ACTUALLY A "TURN OFF" (TO HEAR THE BUILDER'S STORY IN THE FIRST FEW MINUTES) FOR THE LARGE MAJORITY OF BUYERS. THE GOOD NEWS IS THAT MOST "MASTER CLOSERS" AND EXCELLENT SALES PEOPLE KNOW THIS AND DON'T PRACTICE THIS IN THE REAL WORLD.

THE BAD NEWS IS THAT WHEN THE MASTER CLOSER GETS SHOPPED AND IF THEY ARE NOT AWARE THEY ARE BEING SHOPPED, THEY "READ THE BUYER" AND DON'T ALWAYS GET "GOOD GRADES" ON THEIR SHOP, BUT THEY SELL MORE THAN ANYONE ELSE. WHICH IS MORE IMPORTANT?

SOME COMPANIES ARE "INSISTING" THAT THIS BUILDER'S STORY GOES ON FOR ABOUT FIVE MINUTES RIGHT IN THE BEGINNING. LET'S GET REAL! YES, THERE IS A TIME AND PLACE FOR THE "BUILDER'S STORY" BUT NOT RIGHT AWAY AND NOT FOR SO LONG.

THE BEST PLACE FOR IT IS IN THE MIDDLE OF THE CRITICAL PATH OF SELLING (DEMONSTRATION-BOX #5).

WHAT ARE YOUR THOUGHTS ON THIS? SEE CHAPTER XXXI.

I HAVE BEEN ABLE TO INFLUENCE SOME OF THE LARGE PUBLIC COMPANIES AND LARGE NATIONAL INDEPENDENT COMPANIES AWAY FROM THIS, BUT I'M STILL WORKING ON IT.

THINGS I AGREE WITH

THINGS I DISAGREE WITH

THINGS I NEED TO WORK ON

ACTION PLAN FOR ME

CHAPTER VII

> **QUESTION #4:** OF ALL THE STEPS OF THE CRITICAL PATH OF SELLING NEW HOMES, THE OUTRIGHT MOST IMPORTANT STEP IS "DEMONSTRATION," IN ORDER TO DIFFERENTIATE THE BUILDER AND THE NEW HOME FROM EXISTING (USED) HOMES AND OTHER COMPETITORS.

LIE/MYTH #4: OF ALL THE STEPS OF THE CRITICAL PATH OF SELLING NEW HOMES, THE OUTRIGHT MOST IMPORTANT STEP IS <u>DEMONSTRATION!</u>

YOU WILL SEE THAT I AM "BIASED" WHEN IT COMES TO SELLING. MY BIAS, NO MATTER WHAT YOU ARE SELLING, IS IN THE DIRECTION OF

CLOSING

I BELIVE "CLOSING" IS ABSOLUTELY THE MOST IMPORTANT STEP OF THE CRITICAL PATH OF SELLING

THESE ARE NOT CHARLES J. CLARKE III'S CRITICAL PATH STEPS. THESE ARE CRITICAL PATH STEPS THAT ARE OVER 100 YEARS OLD AND DATE BACK TO SELLING DURING THE INDUSTRIAL REVOLUTION IN THE LATE 1800'S.

OLD GENERIC CRITICAL PATH OF SELLING

1 - MEET AND GREET

2 - QUALIFY
QUALIFY FOR
- READY
- WILLING
- ABLE

3 - DEMONSTRATION OF PRODUCT

4 - SELECTION PROCESS   WHAT DO THEY LIKE BEST

5 - OVERCOME OBJECTIONS AND CLOSE THE SALE

CRITICAL PATH OF SALES AS IT RELATES TO THE BUILDING INDUSTRY

- 1 - MEET AND GREET – MY TAKE ON IT IS, MEET & GREET AND CONNECT WITH THEIR BOLT™, THEIR ANIMAL PERSONALITY. (PACE AND MIRROR WITH THEM.)

- 2 - QUALIFY FOR
- READY: (HAVE THEY DECIDED TO MOVE OR ARE AT LEAST THINKING ABOUT IT?) ABOUT 25% ARE JUST "LOOKERS" AND REALLY HAVEN'T DECIDED TO MOVE. (LAMBS AND OWLS)
- WILLING: WILLING IS ALL ABOUT PRODUCT (HOME AND COMMUNITY). PRODUCT ALSO INCLUDES THE SALESPERSON.
- ABLE: (FINANCIALLY ABLE)

-3 - DEMONSTRATION (EXPLANATION OF PRODUCT) DEMONSTRATION IS THE "3RD STEP" OF THE CRITICAL PATH. THIS IS WHY IT REALLY DOES NOT MAKE SENSE FROM A CRITICAL PATH PERSPECTIVE TO TELL THE BUILDER STORY IN THE FIRST FEW MINUTES. TELL IT <u>LATER</u>, UNDER DEMONSTRATION.

THERE ARE STILL A LOT OF NEW HOME SALES PEOPLE WHO JUST "JUMP IN" AND START TALKING ABOUT THEIR HOMES. WORSE YET IS THE PRESENTATION THAT SAYS GO TAKE A LOOK AT OUR MODEL (WITHOUT QUALIFYING AT ALL.) (THESE SALES PEOPLE USUALLY HAVE A CLOSING RATIO OF A "CLERK" OR "BAD CLERK.")

-4 - SELECTION
SELECTION OF THE HOME (FLOOR PLAN) AND HOME SITE (IF NOT AN ON-YOUR-LOT BUILDER)
- HOW DO YOU LIKE OUR COMMUNITY?
- IS THIS A COMMUNITY YOU WOULD LIKE TO LIVE IN?
- WHICH HOME DO YOU LIKE BEST FOR YOUR NEEDS?
- IS THIS A HOME YOU WOULD LIKE TO OWN?

-5 -OVERCOMING OBJECTIONS AND CLOSING THE SALE
USING THE RIGHT CLOSING METHODOLOGY FOR EACH PERSONALITY (KILLER CLOSES FOR EACH PERSONALITY™)

OWLS NEED AND WANT THE MOST DEMONSTRATION, THEN LAMBS. BULLS NEED AND WANT DEMONSTRATIONS THE LEAST. TIGERS NEED DEMONSTRATION THE MOST BUT ALSO WANT IT THE LEAST.

IN MY OPINION, BASED ON WHAT BUYERS HAVE TOLD US THROUGH THE YEARS, SOME BUYERS ACTUALLY FIND IT OFFENSIVE REGARDING HOW MUCH DETAIL IS SPENT BY "OWL" SALESPEOPLE ON "MUNDANE" AND "OVER-DETAILED" PRESENTATIONS.

"THIS IS THE KITCHEN" – (DUH!)

WE ACTUALLY HAVE ON OUR "MYSTERY SHOPS," STATEMENTS BY A FEW SALESPEOPLE AS THEY STEP INTO THE KITCHEN, "THIS IS THE KITCHEN," AND AS THEY GO INTO THE BATHROOM, "THIS IS THE BATHROOM."

WE HAVE PROBABLY ALL EXPERIENCED THAT, HAVEN'T WE?

BULLS HAVE A HIGH PROBABILITY OF WANTING TO SEE THE MODEL ON THEIR OWN (OFTEN MENTIONING) "I JUST WANT TO SEE IT ON MY OWN." WE CAN SAY SOMETHING LIKE "IF IT'S ALL RIGHT WITH YOU, I WOULD LIKE TO START YOU OFF BY DEMONSTRATING SOME SPECIFIC CONSTRUCTION THAT WE DO, AND OUR ATTENTION TO DETAIL. AFTER THAT, I CAN LEAVE YOU ALONE. WOULD THAT BE ALL RIGHT?"

THEN SOME OF THE BULLS WILL ACTUALLY "ALLOW" YOU TO STAY WITH THEM, SOMETIMES KEEPING THEIR DISTANCE.

IF YOU GIVE THE EXACT "WORD FOR WORD" DEMONSTRATION OF YOUR PRODUCT THAT IS OFTEN RECOMMENDED, YOU WILL SOUND LIKE A "ROBOT" AND BE BUSTED BY BULLS FOR DOING THAT.

YES, DEMONSTRATION OF NEW HOMES IS OF COURSE VERY IMPORTANT, YET YOU COULD HAVE THE BEST DEMONSTRATION EVER, BUT IF YOU DON'T CLOSE, IT'S ALL FOR "NAUGHT."

"ALL" THE STEPS OF THE CRICITAL PATHS ARE IMPORTANT, BUT THE MOST IMPORTANT IS THE CLOSING.

YOUR THOUGHTS?

NOTES

THINGS I AGREE WITH

THINGS I DISAGREE WITH

THINGS I NEED TO WORK ON

ACTION PLAN FOR ME

CHAPTER VIII

> **QUESTION #5:** IT WOULD BE TOO PUSHY 100% OF THE TIME, TO ASK FOR THE SALE. YES/NO

MYTH #5: IT WOULD BE TOO PUSHY 100% OF THE TIME, TO ASK FOR THE SALE.

ALMOST EVERY SALES MANAGER THROUGHOUT THE WORLD STRESSES TO THEIR SALES STAFF "ASK EVERYONE FOR THE SALE." (CLOSE EVERYONE)

HOWEVER WHEN COMPANIES DO MYSTERY SHOPPING *(WHETHER THEY USE OUR MYSTERY SHOPPING COMPANY OR NOT)* THE

> **ABSOLUTE MOST NEGLECTED STEP IS <u>CLOSING</u>**

QUESTION "DID THE SALESPERSON ASK YOU TO BUY?"

ANSWER "NO"

AGAIN:

> **IN MY BIASED OPINION, CLOSING IS ABSOLUTELY THE SINGLE MOST IMPORTANT AND NEGLECTED STEP IN SELLING. YES, ALL THE STEPS IN THE CRITICAL PATH ARE IMPORTANT, BUT THE MOST IMPORTANT IS <u>CLOSING.</u>**

WHAT ARE <u>YOUR</u> THOUGHTS ON THIS?

IN THIS CHAPTER, I AM GOING TO TRY TO "CLOSE" ON YOU TO DO A CERTAIN TASK FOR 90 DAYS. THEN IF IT WORKS, YOU CAN "RE-UP" FOR MORE COMMITMENT.

HERE IS WHAT I'M ASKING YOU TO COMMIT. (SOME OF YOU WILL/SOME OF YOU WON'T. THAT'S OKAY.)

WILL YOU COMMIT TO ASK <u>EVERYONE, ALL THE TIME, NO EXCEPTIONS, ALWAYS!</u> (FOR 90 DAYS)

> # "WHAT DO YOU THINK ABOUT GOING AHEAD WITH THIS TODAY™?"

(WITH A LAMB AND TIGER YOU CAN SUBSTITUTE THE WORD "FEEL" INSTEAD OF "THINK.")

I RAN ACROSS SOMEONE'S WEBSITE WHO SOMETIMES GIVES ADVICE TO THE HOMEBUILDING INDUSTRY AND HE MADE THE STATEMENT ONLINE, THE WORST CLOSE IS "WHAT DO YOU THINK ABOUT GOING AHEAD WITH THIS TODAY?"

HE WENT ON TO SAY THAT A PERSON OR COUPLE BUYS A NEW HOME WITH "FEELING, NOT THINKING" (SEE QUESTION #22 AND LIE/MYTH #22)

WHAT HE WAS EXPRESSING WAS HIS LACK OF KNOWLEDGE OF PERSONALITY SELLING™. OWLS AND BULLS <u>PREFER</u> THE WORD "THINK." THAT'S HOW THEY "SORT DATA," BY THINKING. EVEN LAMBS AND TIGERS "THINK" ABOUT BUYING.

IT'S REALLY NOT THAT BIG OF A DEAL IF YOU USE "THINK" OR "FEEL." WHAT I'M SUGGESTING IS THE BIG DEAL IS ASKING THE POTENTIAL BUYER "<u>WHAT DO YOU THINK ABOUT GOING AHEAD WITH THIS TODAY™?</u>" 100% OF THE TIME FOR THE NEXT 90 DAYS. (SUBSTITUTING "FEEL" WHEN IT IS APPROPRIATE, IF YOU "THINK" THAT IS NECESSARY.)

WILL YOU DO THAT?

SALESPEOPLE WHO <u>HAVE</u> DONE THIS AND WHO <u>ARE</u> DOING THIS SEE THEIR SALES IMMEDIATELY INCREASE.

LET ME QUALIFY MORE WHAT I'M SUGGESTING. I CALL THESE MY <u>FIVE MAGIC QUESTIONS™</u>, TO ASK EVERYONE BEFORE THEY LEAVE OR USUALLY ABOUT 20 MINUTES INTO THE PRESENTATION.

1) HOW DO YOU LIKE OUR COMMUNITY?
2) IS THIS A COMMUNITY YOU WOULD LIKE TO LIVE IN?

(*IN "ON YOUR LOT" SALES YOU OF COURSE WOULD NOT ASK THESE COMMUNITY QUESTIONS.)

3) WHICH ONE OF OUR HOMES DO YOU LIKE THE BEST?

4) IS THIS A HOME YOU WOULD LIKE TO OWN?

5) WHAT DO YOU THINK ABOUT GOING AHEAD WITH THIS TODAY? (THE SILVER BULLET™)

THE "FIVE MAGIC QUESTIONS™" AND "THE SILVER BULLET™" ARE TRADEMARKS OF CHARLES J. CLARKE III

HAVE FUN WITH IT! ASK EVERYONE. "MAKE IT A HABIT."

EMAIL US AT CHARLES@PERSONALITYSELLING.COM IF YOU WANT TO RECEIVE A FREE "TENT CARD," SO YOU CAN PUT IT ON YOUR DESK. ON THE INSIDE WILL BE DETAILED "KILLER CLOSES FOR EACH PERSONALITY™."

LET ME ASK YOU A QUESTION. "DID YOU BRUSH YOUR TEETH TODAY? WHY?" SURE IT'S BECAUSE IT IS GOOD HYGIENE AND BECAUSE YOUR TEETH WILL BE WHITER AND YOUR BREATH WILL BE BETTER, AND YOU WILL KEEP YOUR TEETH LONGER. HOWEVER, YOU ALSO DO IT BECAUSE "<u>IT IS A HABIT</u>."

MAKE THIS A HABIT!

THE CHARLES CLARKE COMMITMENT™

I _____ HEREBY COMMIT TO ASK, "WHAT DO YOU THINK ABOUT GOING AHEAD WITH THIS TODAY," 100% OF THE TIME, ALL OF THE TIME, WITH EVERYONE, (NO EXCEPTIONS) FOR THE NEXT 90 DAYS BEGINNING_____.

(MONTH/DATE/YEAR)

_____   _____   _____   _____

_____

    SIGNED   COMPANY   CITY   STATE

     DATE

YOUR EMAIL ADDRESS_____ YOUR PHONE NUMBER _____

MAKE A COPY OF THIS PAGE*

GIVE A COPY TO YOUR SALES MANAGER AND EMAIL A COPY TO CHARLES CLARKE III.

EMAIL= CHARLES@PERSONALITYSELLING.COM

CHARLES' CELL PHONE = (678)516-4833

*THIS IS THE ONLY PAGE IN THIS BOOK THAT YOU HAVE MY WRITTEN PERMISSION TO COPY.

QUIT TRYING TO SECOND GUESS IF IT'S THE RIGHT THING TO DO. JUST DO IT, WITH EVERYONE!

AS MANY OF YOU KNOW AND AS I HAVE ALREADY MENTIONED, I AM A BEHAVIORAL SCIENTIST AND WAS A UNIVERSITY INSTRUCTOR AND COLLEGE PROFESSOR. I WANT TO GIVE YOU A LITTLE "PRIVATE" (NOT SO PRIVATE) "COUCH TIME."

HERE ARE 7 PSYCHOLOGICAL REASONS WHY YOU MIGHT NOT NOW OR WOULDN'T BE ASKING THE "FIVE MAGIC QUESTIONS™"

1) "**FEAR OF REJECTION**" (YOU ALSO THINK IT WOULD BE "STUPID" TO DO THIS IN SOME CASES.) (GET OVER IT!)

2) "I DON'T WANT TO BE TOO PUSHY." (GET OVER IT!)

3) MY "JUDGMENT" IS THAT THEY ARE NOT READY TO BE ASKED (THEY EVEN TOLD ME THAT): (BULLS ARE THE MOST JUDGMENTAL AS SALESPEOPLE)

   A) THEY WEREN'T A BUYER (NOT READY)
   B) DIDN'T LIKE THE HOME (NOT WILLING)
   C) DIDN'T HAVE THE MONEY (NOT ABLE)
   D) NEEDED TO SELL THEIR HOME
   E) THOUGHT THE PRICE WAS TOO HIGH
   F) SPOUSE WASN'T THERE
   G) NEEDED TO THINK IT OVER

"PAD" THE OBJECTIONS, SO THEY UNDERSTAND YOU HEARD THE OBJECTION. "I REALLY DID HEAR YOU SAY YOU NEEDED TO SELL YOUR HOME BUT I'M COMPELLED TO ASK YOU ANYWAY, 'WHAT DO YOU THINK ABOUT GOING AHEAD WITH THIS TODAY?'"

4) **I'M NOT READY** (I DIDN'T GET A CHANCE TO GIVE MY FULL PRESENTATION)("I" WOULDN'T BUY UNDER THESE CIRCUMSTANCES)

5) I THINK THEY WILL "BE BACK"

> (THE "BE BACK BUS" DOESN'T STOP HERE IF THEY MEET A CLOSER ALONG THE WAY.)

6) I DIDN'T FEEL LIKE IT (IT'S JUST NOT MY STYLE) (THAT'S NOT HOW I ROLL) (GET OVER IT!)

7) I JUST PLAIN "FORGOT" TO ASK (THAT'S WHY YOU NEED THE TENT CARD.)

GO THROUGH THESE SEVEN AND RANK ORDER THE TOP 3 THAT GET IN YOUR WAY THE MOST. WHAT IS YOUR #1, #2 AND #3? WRITE THEM DOWN, SO YOU CAN OVERCOME THESE REASONS. OFTEN A PERSON'S BULL, OWL, LAMB AND TIGER® SHOWS UP IN TERMS OF THE REASON THEY DON'T ASK.

IN MY PERSONAL TAILOR-MADE SEMINARS FOR COMPANIES I ASK WHICH GETS IN YOUR WAY THE MOST. LAMBS AND OWLS HAVE NUMBERS 1 AND 2 SHOW UP THE MOST, IN THEIR TOP THREE AND SOMETIMES #6.

BULLS HAVE #3 SHOW UP THE MOST (USUALLY). IT'S THEIR #1 REASON BECAUSE BULLS ARE SO OPINIONATED THAT THEY THINK THEY ARE ALWAYS RIGHT.

OWLS HAVE #4 SHOW UP THE MOST IN THEIR TOP THREE.

ALL FOUR ANIMALS HAVE #5 SHOW UP.

TIGERS HAVE #7 SHOW UP THE MOST

> **LET'S LOOK AT REASON #5 "THEY WILL BE BACK."**

WHAT IS YOUR "BEEN BACK™" RATIO? NOT YOUR "BE BACK" RATIO, BUT YOUR "BEEN BACK™" RATIO.

ALLOW ME TO DIGRESS THEN I WILL ANSWER THAT. A "BE BACK" IS, OF COURSE, SOMEONE WHO SAYS THEY WILL BE BACK AND THEY DO COME BACK. MOST COMPANIES USE A "BE BACK" RATIO IN TERMS OF CALCULATING RETURN VISITS. THE AVERAGE "BE BACK" RATIO (RETURN VISITS) WITH COMPANIES APPEARS TO BE ABOUT 20%. THE REASON FOR THIS BEING SO HIGH IS BECAUSE "BE BACKS" CAN BE COUNTED TWICE, OR 3, 4 OR 5 TIMES IF THE PROSPECTIVE BUYER KEEPS RETURNING.

"BEEN BACK™" RATIOS IS A TRADEMARK OF CHARLES J. CLARKE III

WHICH ANIMAL PERSONALITIES DO YOU THINK RETURN THE MOST? THE LEAST?

LAMBS AND OWLS RETURN THE MOST. BULLS USUALLY ONLY COME BACK POSSIBLY ONE MORE TIME, TO JUST CHECK TO SEE IF THEY CAN GET A BETTER PRICE.

TIGERS VERY RARELY EVER COME BACK AT ALL. THEY "PREFER" TO BUY THE FIRST DAY.

DO YOU BELIEVE THAT?

IF YOU ARE AN OWL I KNOW YOU REALLY DON'T BELIEVE THAT, AT THIS POINT IN TIME.

ASK TIGERS!

"BEEN BACK™" RATIO'S

WHERE "BE BACKS" CAN BE COUNTED MORE THAN ONCE, A "BEEN BACK™" IS ONLY COUNTED ONCE.

IF YOU HAVE 100 PEOPLE COME IN (NO MATTER HOW LONG IT TAKES FOR THAT NUMBER TO COME IN), HOW MANY OF THOSE 100 WILL EVER COME BACK?

PLEASE WRITE THIS NUMBER DOWN. TAKE A MOMENT TO THINK ABOUT IT, BUT WRITE SOME NUMBER DOWN BEFORE YOU PROCEED. TURN THAT INTO A PERCENTAGE SINCE IT WAS BASED ON 100.

IN OUR SEMINARS, SOME SALESPEOPLE (NOT MANY) ANSWER THAT THEY THINK THEY HAVE 50%+ "BEEN BACKS.™"

OFTEN (DEPENDING ON COMPANIES) THE MAJORITY ANSWER IS BETWEEN 30% AND 50%.

THE NATIONAL AVERAGE (AS FAR AS WE CAN DISCERN) OF "BEEN BACK™" RATIOS IS 8% TO 10%.

OUT OF EVERY 100 PEOPLE, 90% TO 92% NEVER RETURN. AS MENTIONED SOME OF THE "BE BACKS" COME BACK EVEN 5 OR 6 TIMES, SO A SALESPERSON STARTS TO THINK THAT THEY HAVE MORE "BEEN BACKS"™ THAN THEY REALLY DO.

90% to 92% NEVER COME BACK

AGAIN IN MY SEMINARS, SOME SALESPEOPLE PROFESSIONALLY "DEBATE" THESE "BEEN BACK™" NUMBERS SAYING "I HAVE TWICE THAT MANY OF 8% AND 10%."

READJUSTED, THAT STILL MEANS 80% TO 84% ARE NEVER COMING BACK!

OK! LET'S SAY YOU DO HAVE A 16% TO 20% "BEEN BACK"™ RATIO.

DOES THAT CONVINCE YOU THAT YOU SHOULD BE ASKING EVERYONE: "WHAT DO YOU THINK ABOUT GOING AHEAD WITH THIS TODAY?"

WHAT DO YOU HAVE TO LOSE?

THE ANSWER IS THAT YOU HAVE "NOTHING TO LOSE" EXCEPT OF COURSE THE SALE.

YOU HAVE EVERYTHING TO WIN BY ASKING IT.

WILL YOU MAKE (SIGN) THE COMMITMENT ON THE PREVIOUS PAGE OR HAVE YOU ALREADY SIGNED IT?

GIVE A COPY TO YOUR SALES MANAGER AND SEND US A COPY OF YOUR COMMITMENT ALONG WITH YOUR "THOUGHTS" ABOUT THIS.

FOOTNOTE: TIGERS REALLY DON'T CARE ABOUT ALL THESE PERCENTAGES AND PROBABLY SKIPPED OVER THIS.

THINGS I AGREE WITH

THINGS I DISAGREE WITH

THINGS I NEED TO WORK ON

ACTION PLAN FOR ME

CHAPTER IX

IF YOU ORIGINALLY PUT "YES" TO THIS, WHAT WERE YOUR REASONS?

> **QUESTION #6:** IT IS "VERY RARE" FOR SOMEONE TO "BUY" (GIVE A CHECK AND SIGN A CONTRACT), THE FIRST TIME THEY SEE THE COMMUNITY OR HOME IN PERSON. YES/NO

LIE/MYTH #6: "IT IS RARE FOR SOMEONE TO "BUY" (GIVE A CHECK AND SIGN THE CONTRACT) THE FIRST TIME THEY SEE THE HOME OR COMMUNITY IN PERSON."

WERE YOUR REASONS SOMETHING LIKE:

- 1 - "PEOPLE DON'T BUY THE FIRST DAY"
- 2 - "THEY NEED MORE INFORMATION AND RESEARCH TO MAKE SUCH A BIG DECISION."
- 3 - "THERE'S TOO MUCH COMPETITION OUT THERE FOR PEOPLE TO CHOOSE FROM."
- 4 - "IT RARELY HAPPENS."

ACTUALLY THE MAIN REASON WHY YOU MIGHT HAVE SAID "YES" TO IT BEING "RARE" WAS BECAUSE YOU WOULDN'T DO IT THE FIRST DAY AND YOU WOULD NEED MORE TIME AND RESEARCH. YOU THINK IT'S ABOUT YOU, NOT THEM, AND IT REALLY SHOULD BE IN REVERSE (ABOUT THEM AND NOT YOU).

IF YOU WOULD NOT BUY THE FIRST DAY, YOU PROBABLY WILL NOT BELIEVE THIS. (I HAVE ALREADY MENTIONED THIS.)

> **APPROXIMATELY 50% OF ALL THE POPULATION WE SURVEY, SAY THEY HAVE BOUGHT A HOME THE FIRST DAY OR WOULD PREFER TO BUY THE FIRST DAY. (TIGERS AND BULLS)**

DO YOU BELIEVE THAT?

SOME BUYERS SAY THEY DIDN'T BUY BECAUSE EITHER THE SALESPERSON DIDN'T ASK THEM OR THAT THE SALESPERSON <u>CONVINCED</u> THEM NOT TO. "TAKE YOUR TIME, THERE IS NO NEED TO RUSH INTO THIS."

YOUR THOUGHTS?

> YOU DON'T GET MANY SALES DONE THE FIRST DAY THEY ARE IN, BECAUSE YOU ARE NOT EXPECTING IT.

> **IF AT LEAST 33% OF YOUR TOTAL SALES ARE <u>NOT</u> DONE THE FIRST DAY YOU MIGHT BE (PROBABLY ARE) MISSING <u>ALL</u> THE TIGERS AND A GOOD PORTION OF THE BULLS.**

REMEMBER, A GOOD MIND SET IS THAT THE POPULATION IS DIVIDED INTO ABOUT 25% BULLS, 25% OWLS, 25% LAMBS & 25% TIGERS.

SEE THE LETTER FROM JOHN CRISTY, ON THE NEXT PAGE.

SEND US <u>YOUR</u> TESTIMONIALS TO BE INCLUDED IN MY NEXT BOOK.

> **APPROXIMATELY 1/3+ OF ALL YOUR SALES "COULD BE"/"SHOULD BE" DONE THE FIRST DAY, AND THAT IS "NOT RARE."**

To: Charles Clarke III

From: John Christy

Subject: Thank You

Hello Charles,

It was great to see you again. I just wanted to take a moment and Thank You for sharing your philosophy of selling which has impacted my selling career. During what most would consider turbulent times I was able to sell 88 homes during the past year.

It was a mix of townhouses and detached single family ranging in price from $170,000-$300,000. My conversion ratio on the townhome mix was 1 out of 3 and in the detached single family it ended up being 1 out of 6. And it will come as no surprise to you that 37% of these customers purchased on the first day, just like you recommend.

If I were to have listened to the old myths like:

1) "You have to earn the right to close,"
2) Tell the Builder Story first before you qualify,
3) "People don't buy the first day,"
4) "Everyone wants a relationship," etc.

I would have not sold even half the amount of homes I did, listening to traditional myths.

Charles you are truly the Master Professor who helped turn me into another one of your Master Closers. Your methodology has empowered me to shorten my sales cycle and create a high level customer experience, because I now take the time to relate to each individual's personality (their BOLT™).

Thanks again to you and my Sales Manager Briggs Napier for providing you to me, and for training material that actually makes a difference in the bottom line of the student not just the teacher.

Looking forward to another great year. YO LET'S DO IT!

Expect Success!

John J. Christy

Raleigh, N.C.

88 homes sold in one year

THINGS I AGREE WITH

THINGS I DISAGREE WITH

THINGS I NEED TO WORK ON

ACTION PLAN FOR ME

CHAPTER X

> **QUESTION #7:** IF PEOPLE ARE MARRIED THEY WOULD <u>NOT</u> "BUY" IF THEIR SPOUSE IS NOT THERE. YES/NO

LIE/MYTH #7: IF PEOPLE ARE MARRIED, THEY WOULD <u>NOT</u> BUY IF THEIR SPOUSE IS NOT THERE.

SOME OF THE "ARGUMENTS" THAT PEOPLE SAY WHEN THEY AGREE WITH THIS MYTH ARE:

IF I BOUGHT A HOUSE WITHOUT MY SPOUSE'S APPROVAL, MY SPOUSE WOULD WANT TO DIVORCE ME.

THAT'S WHY I SUGGEST (IF NEEDED) WRITE THE CONTRACT (PURCHASE AGREEMENT) "SUBJECT TO SPOUSE'S APPROVAL."

BULLS AND TIGERS (MALE AND FEMALE) SAY THEY WOULD HAVE NO PROBLEM SIGNING A CONTRACT WITHOUT THEIR SPOUSE BEING THERE (AND REMAIN MARRIED).

OWL AND LAMB BUYERS HAVE A HIGHER PROBABILITY OF <u>NOT</u> DOING THIS.

HERE IS WHAT I'M SUGGESTING. IF <u>YOU</u> WOULD NOT BUY A HOME WITHOUT YOUR SPOUSE BEING THERE, EVEN WITH A "SUBJECT TO SPOUSE'S APPROVAL," THEN <u>YOU</u> PROBABLY HAVE THE "VOODOO WHAMMY" IN YOUR SUBCONSCIOUS BRAIN AND WOULD HAVE A HIGHER PROBABILITY OF <u>NOT WANTING TO ASK,</u> "WHAT DO YOU THINK ABOUT GOING AHEAD WITH THIS TODAY?"

I SAY "GET OVER IT" AND ASK ANYWAY!

EXAMPLE OF GENERAL NORMAN SCHWARZKOPF (WHO HAS SINCE PASSED AWAY):

A NUMBER OF YEARS AGO I WAS TOLD BY A CUSTOM BUILDER IN A GATED COMMUNITY IN TAMPA, FLORIDA, THAT GENERAL NORMAN SCHWARZKOPF BOUGHT A MULTI-MILLION DOLLAR HOME FROM THEM THE VERY FIRST DAY THE GENERAL WAS IN.

THE CUSTOM BUILDER'S SALESPERSON HAD JUST BEEN THROUGH MY 3-DAY MASTER CLOSER TRILOGY™ AND SHE ASKED THE FIVE MAGIC QUESTIONS AND THE GENERAL AFTER QUESTION #5, SAID "YES." HIS WIFE WAS NOT THERE AND THERE WAS <u>NO</u> "SUBJECT TO WIFE'S APPROVAL." THE SALES LADY WAS "BLOWN AWAY" THAT THE GENERAL SAID "YES!" NO ONE HAD EVER BOUGHT FROM HER THE FIRST DAY IN THIS MULTI-MILLION DOLLAR COMMUNITY, MUCH LESS WITHOUT THEIR SPOUSE BEING THERE. ("TRUE/TRUE" STORY) TRUTH CODE FOR "IT REALLY HAPPENED" (PROMISE/PROMISE)

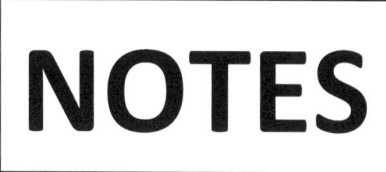

THINGS I AGREE WITH

THINGS I DISAGREE WITH

THINGS I NEED TO WORK ON

ACTION PLAN FOR ME

CHAPTER XI

> **QUESTION #8:** CROSSED ARMS AND NO SMILE MEANS THAT A PERSON IS DEFENSIVE. YES/NO

LIE/MYTH #8: CROSSED ARMS AND NO SMILE MEANS THAT A PERSON IS **DEFENSIVE.**

CROSS YOUR ARMS IN FRONT OF YOU RIGHT NOW. TAKE THE SMILE OFF YOUR FACE. LOOK IN THE MIRROR. WHAT DOES IT LOOK LIKE TO YOU? IF YOU ARE A BULL, YOU'RE NOT GOING TO TAKE ME UP ON LOOKING IN THE MIRROR, BECAUSE YOU KNOW IT'S WHAT <u>YOU</u> DO

THAT STANCE OF CROSSED ARMS, WITH NO SMILE, ("BULL BODY LANGUAGE") ACTUALLY IS A <u>"BUYING SIGN"</u> FOR THE BULL MAN & BULL WOMAN, AND IT IS COMFORTABLE FOR THEM.

THIS TIGHT BODY LANGUAGE POSITION (ARMS CROSSED) HAS BEEN WRITTEN ABOUT IN OTHER BOOKS AND HAS BEEN SPOKEN ABOUT IN SEMINARS AS BEING NEGATIVE.

BULLS WILL TELL YOU THAT IT IS A VERY <u>COMFORTABLE</u>, NATURAL POSITION AND IT MEANS THEY ARE PAYING ATTENTION (A BUYING SIGN/NOT DEFENSIVE).

I RECENTLY SAW A SEGMENT OF BILL O'RILEY'S "THE NO-SPIN ZONE" AND HE HAD ON A SO CALLED "BODY LANGUAGE EXPERT" WHO WAS ANALYZING A CLIP OF A WELL-KNOWN BULL LADY IN HER "BULL STANCE" AND THIS "EXPERT" POINTED OUT HOW THIS MEANT THAT THIS BULL LADY WAS BEING COMPLETELY DEFENSIVE. NOT SO! SHE WAS JUST BEING A CONTENT BULL.

"MISREADING" A PERSON'S BODY LANGUAGE CAN EQUATE TO LOSING A SALE.

QUICK CLIP-MORE ON BODY LANGUAGE

OWLS PERCH WITH NO SMILE

PUT YOUR HAND ON YOUR CHIN AND YOUR OTHER ARM UNDER THE ELBOW OF THE HAND ON YOUR CHIN. COME ON PERCH! THAT'S WHAT OWLS DO. IF YOU DID IT NATURALLY YOU'RE PROBABLY AN OWL.

LAMBS HEAD-BOB WITH AN AGREEABLE SMILE.

YOU CAN ASK A LAMB A QUESTION THAT THEY DISAGREE WITH AND WILL SAY "NO," BUT THEIR HEAD IS STILL SAYING "YES" TO YOU, WITH A HEAD-BOB, BUT IT MEANS "NO." THIS CONFUSES BULLS, BUT LAMBS KNOW WHAT I MEAN.

TIGERS TALK A LOT WITH THEIR HANDS AND JUST PLAIN TALK A LOT AND ARE VERY ANIMATED, LIKE CARTOON CHARACTERS.

TIGERS ALSO MOVE AROUND A LOT IF THEY ARE STANDING UP. I CALL IT THE "TIGER DANCE." THEY JUST CONSTANTLY HAVE A STRONG ENERGY CURRENT GOING THROUGH THEM AND ARE HIGHLY EMOTIONAL.

IT'S ALL GOOD!

IT'S JUST ALL DIFFERENT.

BECOME A REAL BODY LANGUAGE EXPERT IN BOLT™.

THINGS I AGREE WITH

THINGS I DISAGREE WITH

THINGS I NEED TO WORK ON

ACTION PLAN FOR ME

CHAPTER XII

> **QUESTION #9:** IT IS VERY IMPORTANT THAT THE SALESPERSON TAKES CONTROL AND MAINTAINS CONTROL THROUGHOUT THE SALES PROCESS, AND THAT THE BUYER IS TOTALLY MADE AWARE OF THIS. YES/NO

LIE/MYTH #9: IT IS VERY IMPORTANT THAT THE SALESPERSON TAKES CONTROL AND MAINTAINS CONTROL THROUGHOUT THE SALES PROCESS, AND THAT THE BUYER IS TOTALLY AWARE THAT THE SALES PERSON IS IN CONTROL.

THIS ONE IS INTERESTING, BECAUSE OFTEN TIMES IT COMES DOWN TO A "BULL FIGHT," WITH THE BULL SALESPERSON AND THE BULL BUYER. EACH ONE WANTING TO BELIEVE THAT THEY ARE THE ONE IN CONTROL, AND WANTING CONTROL

BULL SALESPEOPLE OFTEN PUT "YES" TO THE QUESTION, BUT I AM SUGGESTING THAT THE ANSWER IS "NO."

IF THE BULL BUYER BELIEVES THAT YOU ARE TRYING TO <u>CONTROL</u> THE SITUATION AND YOU MAKE THEM AWARE OF THAT, THE BULL BUYER HIGHLY RESENTS THAT AND OFTEN TIMES WILL ACTUALLY "WALK" OUT ON YOU (LEAVE).

YOU ALWAYS WANT THE BULL BUYER TO <u>BELIEVE</u> THAT "THEY" ARE THE ONE IN CONTROL. WHAT IS WRONG WITH THEM ACTUALLY BEING IN CONTROL AND MAKING THE SALE?

YOUR THOUGHTS?

ONE OF MY PHRASES I RECOMMEND USING <u>AFTER THE QUALIFYING PROCESS</u> IS "HOW WOULD <u>YOU</u> LIKE TO PROCEED?" BULL OWNERS AND SALES MANAGERS HATE IT WHEN I RECOMMEND THAT BECAUSE THEY

SAY THAT WE SHOULD NEVER LET THE BUYER PROCEED THE WAY THEY WANT TO. THEY SAY WE SHOULD PROCEED THE WAY <u>WE</u> WANT TO PROCEED. SURE, DO THAT AND LOSE THE BULL!

AFTER QUALIFYING I RECOMMEND YOU SAY,

"HOW WOULD YOU LIKE TO PROCEED?"

WE COULD NEXT:

- A - SEE THE MODEL (IF YOU HAVE ONE)
- B - GO AND LOOK AT A HOME PLAN THAT YOU DESCRIBED AND FOUND ON THE WEB SITE, THAT IS UNDER CONSTRUCTION
- C - DESCRIBE MORE THE FLOOR PLANS WE HAVE AVAILABLE
- D - ANSWER SOME OF YOUR QUESTIONS, OR
- E - TELL YOU MORE ABOUT OUR BUILDER AND OUR BUILDER'S STORY

SAYING AGAIN: "HOW WOULD YOU LIKE TO PROCEED?"

WHEN YOU DO THIS WHAT DO YOU THINK THE PROBABILITY IS THAT 90%+ CHOOSE TO SEE THE MODEL NEXT?

IF YOU ASK THEM HOW THEY WANT TO PROCEED, LESS THAN 50% WANT TO SEE THE MODEL NEXT.

I KNOW THAT MAY SURPRISE SOME OF YOU, BUT LET'S LOOK AT OUR RESULTS.

BULLS

BULLS HAVE A HIGHER PROBABILITY OF SAYING "LET'S GO LOOK AT THE ACTUAL HOME AND HOME SITE I COULD BUY," AND OFTEN WILL BUY THAT PARTICULAR HOME WITHOUT EVEN WANTING TO SEE THE MODEL (ESPECIALLY IF THE MODEL IS NOT THE FLOOR PLAN IN WHICH THEY ARE INTERESTED.)

OWLS

OWLS HAVE A HIGH PROBABILITY OF NEXT CHOOSING C & D, WANTING TO KNOW MORE ABOUT YOUR FLOOR PLANS (EVEN THOUGH THEY ALREADY SAW THEM ONLINE). THEY ALSO USUALLY HAVE A LIST OF QUESTIONS TO HAVE ANSWERED BEFORE THEY SEE THE MODEL. OWLS HAVE A HIGHER PROBABILITY OF CHOOSING THIS ORDER: C,D,E,A,B

(FLOOR PLAN, QUESTIONS, BUILDER'S STORY, SEEING WHAT IS AVAILABLE, THEN THE MODEL.)

LAMBS

LAMBS WILL PROCEED HOW YOU WANT TO, BUT THEIR PREFERENCE IS SIMILAR TO THE ORDER OF THE OWL.

TIGERS

TIGERS HAVE A HIGHER PROBABILITY OF MAKING THE QUALIFYING PROCESS AS SHORT AS POSSIBLE, AND THEY USUALLY CHOOSE TO SEE THE MODEL NEXT (ABOUT A 95% PROBABILITY*).

TIGER SALESPEOPLE, WHO WOULD THEMSELVES ALWAYS WANT TO SEE THE MODEL RIGHT AWAY, ASSUME THAT <u>EVERYONE</u> WANTS TO DO THE SAME AS THEMSELVES AND JUST START OFF, AFTER <u>BRIEFLY</u> QUALIFYING TO SHOW THE MODEL. PROCEEDING THE WAY <u>THEY</u> WOULD WANT TO PROCEED.

AGAIN:

"WE OFTEN SELL THE WAY WE WOULD LIKE TO BE SOLD AND THUS LOSE ½ TO ¾'S OF OUR POTENTIAL SALES."
CHARLES CLARKE III

YOU NOTICE THAT THROUGHOUT THE BOOK I USE THE REFERENCE TO "PROBABILITY." BULLS, OWLS, LAMBS & TIGERS® IS <u>NOT</u> 100% ACCURATE BUT IT HAS A "PROBABILITY" OF BEING ABOUT 90%+ ACCURATE. WOULDN'T YOU LOVE TO HAVE 90%+ "PROBABILITY" OF WINNING IN LAS VEGAS OR ANY CASINO? THIS SYSTEM GIVES YOU THAT INEVITABLE "PROBABILITY" OF BEING RIGHT AND BECOMING THE "MASTER CLOSER."

How are you going to readjust your own presentation?

THINGS I AGREE WITH

THINGS I DISAGREE WITH

THINGS I NEED TO WORK ON

ACTION PLAN FOR ME

PART 2

CHAPTER	LIE/MYTH	PAGES
XIII	Stating, Restating & Verifying What the Buyer Just Said	65
XIV	Avoiding Talking About the Price Right Away	69
XV	Women Making the Decision of Buying	73
XVI	Creating Urgency	77
XVII	Men Being More Logical & Women Being More Emotional	85
XVIII	Kitchen & Master Bathroom as The Most Important Rooms	87
XIX	Finding Common Ground	93
XX	Memorizing Scripts	95
XXI	10% Closing Ratio	101
XXII	Negotiating	105
XXIII	Follow-Up & Getting Them to Come Back	113

CHAPTER XIII

> **QUESTION #10:** IT IS VERY IMPORTANT TO "ALWAYS STATE, RESTATE AND VERIFY" WHAT THE BUYER JUST SAID. YES/NO

LIE/MYTH #10: IT IS VERY IMPORTANT TO STATE, RESTATE, AND VERIFY WHAT THE BUYER JUST SAID.

SURE! DO THAT IF YOU COMPLETELY WANT TO LOSE THE BULL AND MAKE THE BULL THINK THAT YOU ARE AN IDIOT!

LAST YEAR I WAS WITH A LARGE COMPANY IN SOUTH FLORIDA WHO HAD BROUGHT IN A CONSULTANT WHO RECOMMENDED THIS. WHEN WE DID MYSTERY SHOPPING OF THIS COMPANY, BEFORE I DID MY THREE-DAY MASTER CLOSER SERIES WITH THEM, THIS IS WHAT WE FOUND.

OUR MYSTERY SHOPPER WITNESSED THIS WITH A <u>REAL</u> BUYER.

AFTER GREETING, THE BUYER ASKED FOR A BROCHURE AND A PRICE SHEET.

THE SALESPERSON, WHO HAD BEEN INSTRUCTED TO DO SO BY THE CONSULTANT, SAID "SO YOU ARE SAYING YOU WANT A BROCHURE, IS THAT RIGHT?"

BUYER SAID, "YES! THAT'S WHAT I SAID."

SALESPERSON SAID, "AND YOU ALSO WANT A PRICE SHEET?"

BUYER SAID, "YES! THAT'S WHAT I SAID."

SALESPERSON SAID, "AND YOU WANT A PRICE SHEET BECAUSE?"

BUYER SAID, "SO I KNOW THE PRICE OF YOUR HOMES."

SALESPERSON SAID, "SO THAT MEANS YOU HAVE AN INTEREST IN BUYING ONE OF OUR HOMES?"

BUYER SAID, "I WOULDN'T BE HERE IF I DIDN'T."

IF YOU ARE STILL READING THIS, IT IS "LAUGHABLE" AND VERY SAD. IT IS A "TRUE-TRUE" STORY THAT OCCURRED.

IT CONTINUED ON LIKE THAT EVEN IN THE DEMONSTRATION AND IN A VERY ELABORATE SALES DESIGN CENTER, OUR MYSTERY SHOPPER WITNESSED THAT ABOUT 20 MINUTES INTO THE DESIGN CENTER DEMONSTRATION, WITH ALL THIS STATING, RESTATING AND VERIFYING THAT THE POTENTIAL BUYER ACTUALLY SAID, "IS THIS A JOKE? ARE WE BEING TAPED? AM I GOING TO BE ON YOU TUBE?" THE POTENTIAL BUYER ACTUALLY WALKED OUT.

PLEASE DON'T DO THAT!

BULLS DON'T LIKE AND RESENT ANYTHING BEING STATED, RESTATED AND VERIFIED. ONLY AN OWL WOULD ALLOW THAT WITH NO RESENTMENT.

YOUR THOUGHTS?

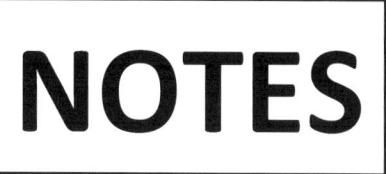

THINGS I AGREE WITH

THINGS I DISAGREE WITH

THINGS I NEED TO WORK ON

ACTION PLAN FOR ME

CHAPTER XIV

> **QUESTION #11:** IF A BUYER ASKS FOR THE PRICE RIGHT AWAY, THE SALESPERSON SHOULD AVOID TELLING THE BUYER THE PRICE RIGHT AWAY AND STAY ON COURSE. YES/NO

LIE/MYTH #11: IF A BUYER ASKS FOR THE PRICE RIGHT AWAY, THE SALESPERSON SHOULD AVOID TELLING THEM THE PRICE RIGHT AWAY AND STAY ON COURSE.

YOU'VE READ BOOKS BEFORE IN GENERAL SELLING AND IN NEW HOME SELLING THAT STATE THIS MYTH AND SOME REALLY BELIEVE IT.

I'M SUGGESTING THAT WHEN A POTENTIAL BUYER ASKS WHAT THE PRICE IS, (NO MATTER WHAT YOU THINK THEIR PERSONALITY IS), GIVE IT TO THEM RIGHT AWAY. THAT'S WHAT THEY WANT! GIVE IT TO THEM.

ON A RECENT MYSTERY SHOP OF OURS, WE HAD THE MYSTERY SHOPPER ASK IN THE FIRST 15 SECONDS AFTER THE MEETING AND GREETING "WHAT IS THE PRICE OF THIS HOME, AS IT IS? (THEY WERE IN A MODEL.)

THE SALESPERSON SAID, "WELL, WE CAN GET TO THAT LATER. THE PRICE WOULDN'T MEAN ANYTHING TO YOU NOW, IF YOU DON'T KNOW ABOUT THE VALUE OF THE HOME AND HOW THE HOME IS BUILT."

AFTER THE SALESPERSON FINISHED HER SENTENCE, OUR MYSTERY SHOPPER REPEATED, "WHAT IS THE PRICE OF THIS HOME? " (JUST LIKE A REAL LIVE BULL BUYER WOULD DO.)

THE SALESPERSON REPEATED HER SENTENCE ABOUT VALUE AND TRIED TO PROCEED. OUR MYSTERY SHOPPER PROCEEDED WITH HIS REAL BULL PERSONALITY AND SAID, "DO YOU KNOW THE PRICE OF THIS HOME, AS IT IS?" SALESPERSON SAID, "YES." OUR MYSTERY SHOPPER SAID, "THEN TELL IT TO ME NOW!"

THE SALESPERSON THEN NERVOUSLY GAVE THE BASE PRICE OF THE HOME AND OUR BULL MYSTERY SHOPPER SAID, "IS THIS THE PRICE OF THIS HOME AS IT IS WITH ALL THE UPGRADES THAT ARE INCLUDED?"

THE SALESPERSON SAID, "NO, THE UPGRADES ARE ABOUT $150,000 MORE."

MYSTERY SHOPPER SAID, "THEN WHY DIDN'T YOU TELL ME THAT WHEN I ASKED WHAT IS THE PRICE OF THE HOME, AS IT IS?"

CAN YOU THE READER FEEL THE FRUSTRATION OF THIS BUYER?

WHY DO WE DO THIS IN OUR INDUSTRY?

WITH A MODEL HOME THERE ARE USUALLY TWO PRICES - THE BASE PRICE AND THE PRICE OF THE HOME, AS IT IS.

LEGITIMATE ANSWER TO "WHAT IS THE PRICE OF THIS HOME?"(IF IT IS A MODEL)

"THE PRICE OF THIS HOME, AS YOU SEE IT, IS $650,000, BUT THE BASE PRICE IS $500,000. IS THIS ABOUT THE PRICE YOU HAD IN MIND? WHAT PRICE RANGE DID YOU HAVE IN MIND WHEN YOU CAME IN?"

I'M SUGGESTING THAT NO MATTER WHAT ANIMAL PERSONALITY YOU ARE WORKING WITH, YOU WANT TO DO THIS.

NO MATTER WHEN IT COMES UP, THERE ARE USUALLY TWO PRICES FOR YOUR MODEL: PRICE AS IT IS AND BASE PRICE. TELL THEM BOTH.

THIS REALLY IS "INTEGRITY SELLING!"

YOUR THOUGHTS? HOW ARE YOU GOING TO READJUST YOUR OWN PRESENTATION?

BULLS & TIGERS HAVE A HIGHER PROBABILITY OF ASKING A DIRECT QUESTION ABOUT THE PRICE RIGHT AWAY.

NOTES

THINGS I AGREE WITH

THINGS I DISAGREE WITH

THINGS I NEED TO WORK ON

ACTION PLAN FOR ME

CHAPTER XV

> **QUESTION #12:** IF A COUPLE IS MARRIED, THE WOMAN ALWAYS MAKES THE FINAL DECISION IN BUYING. YES/NO

> # LIE/MYTH #12: IF A COUPLE IS MARRIED, THE WOMAN **ALWAYS** MAKES THE DECISION IN BUYING.

WHEN I GET TO THIS TOPIC IN MY SEMINARS AND COUNSELING I GET A LOT OF DISAGREEMENT, BECAUSE IT IS SUCH AN INGRAINED MYTH. MOST MARRIAGES THAT ARE INTACT (GOOD MARRIAGES), BOTH THE MAN AND THE WOMAN ARE IN ON THE DECISION. FROM OUR RESEARCH OF ACTUAL BUYERS, IT APPEARS THAT WOMEN MAKE THE DECISION NO MORE THAN 50% TO 60% OF THE TIME. ASK AROUND!

IF THE MAN IS A TIGER OR BULL (THE TWO MORE ASSERTIVE ANIMAL PERSONALITIES,) HE IS PROBABLY THE ONE MAKING THE DECISION, NOT HIS WIFE.

YOUR THOUGHTS?

HERE'S WHAT I THINK HAPPENED OVER 50 YEARS AGO IN OUR INDUSTRY. SOME CONSULTANT STARTED BELIEVING AND SAYING THE WOMAN **ALWAYS** MAKES THE DECISIONS AND OTHER PEOPLE STARTED BELIEVING IT AND PASSED IT ON.

> IT'S JUST NOT TRUE.

CONSEQUENCES OF BELIEVING THIS: IF YOU REALLY BELIEVE THIS YOU WILL GEAR YOUR PRESENTATIONS AND CLOSES TO THE WOMAN AND LOSE THE TIGER/BULL OR BULL/TIGER HUSBAND.

> # SELL TO BOTH! NOT JUST THE WOMAN!

SEVERAL YEARS AGO A NATIONAL BUILDER WHO WAS IN THE TOP 10 OF THE NATION'S LARGEST BUILDERS, TOOK THE IDEA TO HEART THAT THE WOMAN ALWAYS MAKES THE DECISION AND ACTUALLY CHANGED <u>ALL</u> THE STATIONARY TO PINK OR MAUVE TO CONNECT MORE WITH WOMEN. THIS REALLY HAPPENED (TRUE/TRUE.)

WELL, YOU CAN IMAGINE THE RESULTS. IT BACKFIRED ON THEM!

BULL WOMEN FELT THEY WERE BEING PATRONIZED AND BULL MEN COULDN'T UNDERSTAND IT.

THE COLOR THAT IS LIKED THE LEAST BY BULLS IS PINK AND OTHER PASTEL COLORS. YES, OUR RESEARCH SHOWS THAT EACH OF THE ANIMAL PERSONALITIES HAS THEIR FAVORITE AND LEAST FAVORITE COLORS.

THIS BECOMES VERY IMPORTANT IN MERCHANDIZING, BUT IT IS NOT FOR NOW. IT IS A SUBJECT THAT IS COVERED IN DETAIL IN MY BOOK, "BULLS, OWLS, LAMBS & TIGERS® PERSONALITY SELLING™."

BE CAREFUL <u>NOT</u> TO GET SUCKED INTO THIS PAST AND CURRENT MYTH. IT CAN AFFECT YOUR SUCCESSES IN A NEGATIVE WAY.

JUST FOR YOUR EDIFICATION, THE FAVORITE COLORS OF EACH OF THE ANIMAL PERSONALITIES ARE

BULLS	BLACK, DARK BROWN, DARK GREEN (HUNTER'S GREEN)
OWLS	GREY, BEIGE (THE EXCITING COLOR OF BEIGE) (THAT'S OWL HUMOR)
LAMBS	PASTELS-LIGHT BLUE, LIGHT YELLOW, LIGHT GREEN AND PINK (WHICH IS MORE GENDER-BASED)
TIGERS	RED, ORANGE, PURPLE, JEWEL TONES, AND PRIMARY COLORS

REMEMBER THESE ARE "PROBABILITY STATEMENTS" WITH 30 YEARS OF OUR RESEARCH.

THINGS I AGREE WITH

THINGS I DISAGREE WITH

THINGS I NEED TO WORK ON

ACTION PLAN FOR ME

CHAPTER XVI

> **QUESTION #13:** EVEN IF THERE IS NOT AN URGENT SITUATION, THEN THE SALESPERSON NEEDS TO CREATE "URGENCY," IN ORDER TO MOTIVATE THE BUYER. YES/NO

LIE/MYTH #13: EVEN IF THERE IS <u>NOT</u> AN URGENT SITUATION, THE SALESPERSON NEEDS TO CREATE "URGENCY" IN ORDER TO MOTIVATE THE BUYER.

THE ABOVE STATEMENT IS SO UNTRUE AND IS A VERY DETRIMENTAL MIND-SET.

I HEAR FROM BUILDERS ALL THE TIME WHEN I FIRST START WORKING WITH THEIR COMPANY, "PLEASE HELP OUR SALESPEOPLE FIND THE URGENCY OF GOING AHEAD WITH THIS TODAY."

APPROXIMATELY ½ OF THE POPULATION (LAMBS & OWLS) ARE REALLY "TURNED OFF" AND WILL NOT BUY WITH URGENCY CLOSES AND TAKE-AWAY CLOSES.

TAKE-AWAY CLOSE – TAKING IT AWAY FROM THEM. "MAYBE THIS $700,000 COMMUNITY IS <u>NOT</u> FOR YOU. MAYBE YOU SHOULD LOOK AT A LESS EXPENSIVE COMMUNITY." THAT WOULD BE A MOTIVATOR FOR TIGERS AND BULLS AND A "DE-MOTIVATOR" FOR LAMBS AND OWLS.

URGENCY CLOSE – APPLYING URGENCY SO THAT IF THE POTENTIAL BUYER DOES NOT BUY TODAY THEY WILL LOSE OUT ON SOMETHING. SUCH AS "THE PRICE IS GOING UP," "OUR DISCOUNT IS ONLY GOOD TODAY," "THE SUN PORCH INCENTIVE EXPIRES AT THE END OF THE MONTH," "SOMEONE ELSE IS LOOKING AT THE SAME HOME," AND "LET'S TAKE A LOOK AT YOUR TWO FAVORITE HOME-SITES BECAUSE IF YOU DON'T BUY YOUR FIRST FAVORITE SITE TODAY IT MIGHT BE GONE TOMORROW."

LAMBS AND OWLS (APPROXIMATELY 50% OF THE POPULATION) TELL US THAT ALL OF THE ABOVE URGENCY CLOSES ARE A "BIG <u>TURN OFF</u>" TO THEM AND WOULD MAKE THEM NOT EVEN COME BACK FOR THE

APPOINTMENT THAT THE SALESPERSON FORCED UPON THEM. ASK LAMBS AND OWLS THAT YOU KNOW IF THIS IS TRUE. IT IS TRUE!

> IF YOU SAY TO A LAMB/OWL, "IF YOU DON'T BUY TODAY, IT MIGHT BE GONE TOMORROW" THE LAMB/OWL HAS A HIGH PROBABILITY OF SAYING SOMETHING LIKE, "QUE SERA SERA," OR "IF IT'S NOT MEANT TO BE" AND "IF IT'S NOT GOD'S WILL IT MIGHT VERY WELL BE GONE TOMORROW," AND" THAT WOULD BE OKAY WITH ME." YOU'VE HEARD THAT BEFORE, HAVEN'T YOU?

TIGERS AND BULLS ARE BIG ADVOCATES OF URGENCY CLOSES BECAUSE THEY WOULD AND DO WORK ON THEM.

> TIGERS AND BULLS RESPOND VERY WELL TO "FEAR OF LOSS." LAMBS AND OWLS DO NOT. LAMBS AND OWLS ARE NOT MOTIVATED BY LOSS BUT ARE MOTIVATED BY GAINS. RIGHT NOW YOU MIGHT NOT SEE A BIG DIFFERENCE BETWEEN THESE TWO.

EXAMPLE

A MAJOR UNIVERSITY CONDUCTED AN EXPERIMENT WITH MOTIVATING HIGH SCHOOL STUDENTS GOING ONTO COLLEGE. IT WAS A LONGITUDINAL EXPERIMENT INTO THE FUTURE, WHICH INVOLVED MANY FACETS.

WHAT STATEMENT BELOW DO YOU THINK WAS MORE MOTIVATIONAL?

A) IF YOU <u>DO</u> GET GOOD GRADES, YOU <u>WILL</u> BE ABLE TO GET INTO A GOOD COLLEGE! (<u>KEY WORDS "DO" AND "WILL."</u>)

OR

B) IF YOU <u>DON'T</u> GET GOOD GRADES, YOU <u>WON'T</u> BE ABLE TO GET INTO A GOOD COLLEGE! (<u>KEY WORDS "DON'T" AND WON'T."</u>)

WRITE DOWN YOUR ANSWER OF WHICH DO <u>YOU</u> THINK WAS MORE MOTIVATIONAL TO THIS GROUP OF 1000 STUDENTS? WHICH MOTIVATES <u>YOU</u> MORE, A OR B? ANSWER IS ON THE NEXT PAGE.

THE ANSWER IS, IT WAS SPLIT ABOUT 50/50. THE POINT IS ABOUT 50% OF PEOPLE ARE MORE MOTIVATED BY NON-URGENCY ("DO/WILL") AND ABOUT 50% ARE MOTIVATED BY URGENCY ("DON'T/WON'T").

BULLS AND TIGERS IN COLLEGE ARE MORE "PROCRASTINATORS." GIVEN A BIG ASSIGNMENT OF A MAJOR PAPER 15 WEEKS IN ADVANCE, WHEN DO TIGERS AND BULLS START WORKING ON IT? MANY TELL US, THE NIGHT BEFORE WITH AN ALL-NIGHTER AND DO A "DARN GOOD JOB OF IT!" I KNEW THIS TO BE TRUE WHEN I WAS A UNIVERSITY INSTRUCTOR AND COLLEGE PROFESSOR.

OWLS AND LAMBS TELL US THEY HAVE A HIGHER PROBABILITY OF WORKING ON IT ALL THROUGH THE SEMESTER AND HAVE IT COMPLETED WAY IN ADVANCE. HOW ABOUT YOU? HOW DOES THIS RELATE TO CLOSING AND URGENCY CLOSES?

> **TIGERS AND BULLS LIKE PRESSURE; LAMBS AND OWLS DON'T. THIS APPLIES TO SALES AS WELL.**

> WE WILL SEE LATER FROM THE "LIES/MYTHS #26 ON OBJECTIONS," THAT THERE ARE HUNDREDS OF OBJECTIONS THAT CAN BE BROKEN DOWN TO ONLY 7 OBJECTIONS.

LAMBS AND OWLS HAVE A HIGHER PROBABILITY OF SAYING, "I WANT TO THINK IT OVER." WHEN LAMBS SAY THIS, BULLS WANT TO APPLY URGENCY AND THUS LOSE THE SALE.

> **IS "I WANT TO THINK IT OVER" A REAL OBJECTION OR A SMOKE SCREEN? GO AHEAD AND ANSWER THAT.**

MORE BULLS AND SOME TIGERS SAY IT'S A "SMOKE SCREEN." I HEARD THE LATE (AND GREAT) ZIG ZIGLER SAY MANY TIMES IN HIS SEMINARS, "WHEN A BUYER SAYS THEY NEED TO THINK IT OVER, IT'S JUST A SMOKE SCREEN." THAT WAS ZIG ZIGLER, A TIGER/BULL, SAYING THAT.

I'M SUGGESTING THAT IF YOU REALLY THINK IT'S A SMOKE SCREEN YOU WILL TREAT IT AS A SMOKE SCREEN AND THUS LOSE THE LAMB. WITH THE LAMB (AND WITH THE OWL) IF YOU "BELIEVE" IT IS ONLY A SMOKE SCREEN YOU REALLY DON'T KNOW WHAT THEY ARE SAYING. BULLS SEE IT AS A SMOKE SCREEN, BECAUSE IF THEY SAID THAT (AND THEY PROBABLY WOULDN'T,) IT COULD BE A SMOKE SCREEN.

> IN 1983 TOMMY HOPKINS AND I HAD A SERIES OF ABOUT THIRTEEN SEMINARS SCHEDULED ALL AROUND THE UNITED STATES. HE HAD AND HAS IN HIS BOOK, "MASTER THE ART OF CLOSING," (WHICH IS STILL IN PRINT, AND I HIGHLY RECOMMEND YOU READ IT,) MANY LISTS OF CLOSES, ONE OF WHICH IS THE **THINK IT OVER CLOSE**

YOU'LL PROBABLY RECOGNIZE A VARIATION OF IT. IT GOES SOMETHING LIKE THIS:

POTENTIAL BUYERS SAY, "I NEED TO THINK IT OVER."

THIS IS OFTEN AFTER POSSIBLY AN HOUR PLUS TOGETHER AND AFTER THE POTENTIAL BUYERS SAID THEY LOVED THE COMMUNITY, IT WAS DEFINITELY A COMMUNITY THEY WANTED TO LIVE IN, THEY REALLY LIKED A PARTICULAR HOME, AND IT WAS A HOME THEY WANTED TO OWN ON THE PARTICULAR HOME-SITE THEY CHOSE.

HOWEVER, WHEN THE SALESPERSON SAYS SOMETHING LIKE, "SO LET'S GO AHEAD WITH THIS TODAY," THE POTENTIAL BUYER SAYS, "NO, I NEED TO THINK IT OVER."

DOES THIS SOUND FAMILIAR?

WHAT TOMMY HOPKINS TAUGHT AND WHAT SOME OTHERS ADVOCATE TODAY, IS SAYING "WHAT DO YOU NEED TO THINK OVER?"

POTENTIAL LAMB BUYER RESPONSE, "EVERYTHING!"

SALESPERSON: "WELL YOU SAID YOU LIKED THE COMMUNITY, THE HOME, THE SITE, AND THE PRICE. WHAT IS IT YOU NEED TO THINK OVER?"

AGAIN THE ANSWER IS, "EVERYTHING."

> SALESPERSON: "IS IT THE COMMUNITY?"
>
> POTENTIAL BUYER: "NO."
>
> "IS IT THE HOME?" RESPONSE, "NO."
>
> "IS IT THE COMMUNITY?" RESPONSE, "NO."
>
> "IS IT THE PRICE?" RESPONSE, "NO."
>
> "IS IT SOMETHING ABOUT ME?" RESPONSE, "NO."
>
> "THEN WHAT IS IT?" RESPONSE, "I JUST NEED TO THINK IT ALL OVER."

> **THE BULL SALESPERSON IS HIGHLY FRUSTRATED BECAUSE THEY WERE USING A CLOSE THAT <u>NEVER</u> WAS DESIGNED TO WORK ON LAMBS AND <u>NEVER HAS!</u>**

> **IN MY OPINION IT IS A FRUSTRATING CLOSE THAT NEVER WORKED ON ANYONE AND HAS CAUSED MANY 1000'S OF SALES TO BE LOST!**

I CALL IT THE "IS IT THE"/"IS IT THE"/"IS IT THE" CLOSE AND IT BUGS EVERYONE. CAN YOU IMAGINE EVER DOING THAT WITH A BULL WHO SAID THEY JUST NEEDED TO THINK IT OVER TO GET ONE OTHER THING DONE? THE BULL WOULD WALK OUT AND THE LAMB WOULD NOT COME BACK FOR THE APPOINTMENT THAT THE BULL FORCED UPON THEM. LAMBS (AND OWLS) DON'T LIKE URGENCY AND "URGENCY CLOSES." PLEASE RE-READ THIS.

> "SO WHAT SHOULD I DO IF A LAMB SAYS, 'I WANT TO THINK IT OVER'?"

> WRITE IT UP "SUBJECT TO THINKING IT OVER FOR 24 HOURS AND APPROVING OF HOME WITHIN 24 HOURS" AND DON'T BADGER THEM.

WRITE IT UP JUST LIKE YOU WOULD IF SOMEONE NEEDED TO BRING THEIR SPOUSE IN TO SEE IT TOMORROW, "SUBJECT TO SPOUSE COMING IN WITHIN 24 HOURS AND APPROVING OF HOME."

IN EACH CASE, YOU WOULD GET A CHECK AND A SIGNED CONTRACT.

IF YOU ARE A BULL SALESPERSON, A BULL SALES MANAGER, OR A BULL OWNER, I DON'T EXPECT YOU TO "GET THIS" OR UNDERSTAND THE REASONS FOR "SUBJECT TO THINKING IT OVER FOR 24 HOURS."

> YOU DON'T HAVE TO "UNDERSTAND IT." JUST DO IT!

> **IF YOU WANT, CONTACT ME PERSONALLY ABOUT THIS FOR MORE EXPLANATION.**

THERE IS AN "ART FORM" TO CLOSE EACH OF THE FOUR ANIMAL PERSONALITIES AND THEIR SPOUSE, WHO IS OFTEN AN OPPOSITE PERSONALITY.

AGAIN IN MY FULL-BLOWN BOOK ON "BULLS, OWLS, LAMBS AND TIGERS®: PERSONALITY SELLING™" AND IN MY 3-DAY MASTER CLOSER SEMINARS, OR EVEN MY 1-DAY SEMINARS, I ANSWER ALL THESE QUESTIONS OF HOW TO SEAMLESSLY CLOSE EACH ANIMAL PERSONALITY.

I'M NOT TRYING TO BE "COY" IN NOT GIVING MORE INFORMATION ON THIS NOW, BUT IT IS REALISTIC THAT I CAN ONLY COVER SO MUCH IN THIS BOOK, "LIES AND MYTHS WE HAVE BEEN TAUGHT IN SELLING NEW HOMES™."

THE PURPOSE HERE IS TO GRAB YOUR ATTENTION IN CONVINCING YOU THAT YOU MAY BE CLOSING ONLY THE WAY <u>YOU</u> WOULD LIKE TO BE CLOSED, THUS LOSING APPROXIMATELY ½ TO ¾'S OF YOUR POTENTIAL SALES. YOU HAVE TO PRACTICE, DRILL AND REHEARSE THIS. (PDR)

THINGS I AGREE WITH

THINGS I DISAGREE WITH

THINGS I NEED TO WORK ON

ACTION PLAN FOR ME

CHAPTER XVII

> **QUESTION #14:** MEN ARE ALWAYS MORE "LOGICAL" IN BUYING A NEW HOME, WHILE WOMEN ARE ALWAYS MORE "EMOTIONAL." YES/NO

> ## LIE/MYTH #14: MEN ARE ALWAYS MORE "LOGICAL" IN BUYING A NEW HOME, WHILE WOMEN ARE ALWAYS MORE "EMOTIONAL."

NOT TRUE!

I THINK YOU PROBABLY SEE THE TREND NOW. BULLS, OWLS, LAMBS AND TIGERS® IS NOT "GENDER BASED" OR "GENDER BIASED." ABOUT 25% OF THE POPULATION IS EACH ANIMAL. THE SAME IS TRUE FOR MALENESS AND FEMALENESS.

HAVE YOU READ OR HEARD OF THE FUN BOOK BY JOHN GRAY, "MEN ARE FROM MARS AND WOMEN ARE FROM VENUS?" THAT BOOK, WHICH I RECOMMEND, IS ABOUT ½ RIGHT. BUT IT IS FUN.

> ## POINT: BULL WOMEN HAVE MORE IN COMMON PERSONALITY-WISE WITH BULL MEN THAN THEY DO WITH LAMB WOMEN.

> ## LAMB WOMEN HAVE MORE IN COMMON WITH LAMB MEN THAN THEY DO WITH BULL WOMEN.

READ THAT AGAIN AND SEE IF YOU WOULD AGREE WITH THAT.

READ JOHN GRAY'S BOOK AND SEE IF YOU DON'T AGREE WITH ABOUT ½ OF HIS PREMISES.

ONE OF THE LAST YEARS AT THE NATIONAL ASSOCIATION OF HOME BUILDERS ANNUAL MEETING I HAD TO LISTEN TO A FEMALE TIGER TALK ABOUT HER HUSBAND (WHO IS AN OWL), ON HOW DIFFERENT THEY WERE. HER CONCLUSION WAS WOMEN ARE MORE EMOTIONAL AND MEN ARE MORE LOGICAL AND THAT'S HOW WE SHOULD ALL TREAT MEN AND WOMEN (BASED SOLELY ON HER OWN EXPERIENCES). DON'T FALL INTO THAT TRAP! IF YOU HAVE FALLEN INTO THIS MYTH IN THE PAST, IT COULD HAVE AFFECTED YOUR SALES IN A NEGATIVE WAY (LOST SALES).

THINGS I AGREE WITH

THINGS I DISAGREE WITH

THINGS I NEED TO WORK ON

ACTION PLAN FOR ME

CHAPTER XVIII

> **QUESTION #15:** THE KITCHEN AND MASTER BATHROOM WERE, AND STILL ARE, THE MOST IMPORTANT ROOMS IN THE NEW HOME FOR THE BUYER. YES/NO

LIE/MYTH #15: THE KITCHEN AND MASTER BATHROOM ARE STILL THE MOST IMPORTANT ROOMS IN THE NEW HOME.

> **YOU CAN SEE THIS LIE/MYTH PRESENTED IN EVERY HUGE ANNUAL KITCHEN AND BATH SHOW. OF COURSE, IT IS SELF-SERVING FOR THEM. (AND THAT'S OK.)**

IT'S JUST NOT TRUE!

DO YOU WANT A QUICK REVIEW OF OUR 30 YEARS OF RESEARCH ON WHAT EACH ANIMAL SAYS IS THEIR FAVORITE ROOM?

GUESS THE FAVORITE ROOMS OR TYPE OF HOME EACH ANIMAL PERSONALITY PREFERS:

BULL _____

OWL _____

LAMB _____

TIGER _____

REMEMBER IT'S BASED ON "PROBABILITY."

IF YOU HAVE NEVER BEEN TO THE NATIONAL KITCHEN AND BATH SHOW, IT IS A "MUST SEE" SPECTACULAR SHOW, AS ARE ALL NAHB SHOWS AND CONVENTIONS. YOU **WILL** LEARN AND MAKE MONEY FROM ATTENDING THEM.

> **BULLS - THE DEN OR "ME" ROOM. BULLS ALSO PREFER THE FOYER-HALLWAY ENTRANCE TO BE GRAND WITH HIGH CEILINGS.**

BULLS ALSO PUT THE MOST EMPHASIS ON THE "ELEVATIONS OF THE HOME" (OUTSIDE APPEARANCE). (DON'T REFER TO THE OUTSIDE APPEARANCE OF THE HOME AS AN ELEVATION -TOO MANY BUYERS (ESPECIALLY TIGERS) STILL THINK THAT MEANS THE NUMBER OF FEET ABOVE SEA LEVEL.)

> **OWLS – IT'S THE OWL WHO PUTS THE MOST EMPHASIS ON THE KITCHEN AND ON THE PRACTICAL LIVING ROOM**

> **LAMBS –THE WARM, COZY, FRIENDLY FAMILY ROOM,** WITH POSSIBLY A FIREPLACE. (YES, EVEN IN WARMER CLIMATES.)

> **TIGERS – THE SENSUAL, SEXY MASTER BEDROOM WITH THE SENSUAL, SEXY MASTER BATH**
>
> - (IN MORE EXPENSIVE HOMES THE <u>SITTING ROOM</u> OFF THE MASTER BEDROOM.)
> - THE MASTER BATHROOM WITH AN "OOOH, BUBBA TUB." ("OOOH, BUBBA. LOOK AT THAT TUB!") THERE'S A LONG STORY ATTACHED TO THAT, BUT NOT FOR NOW.
> - THE SAME BATHTUB THAT OWLS WOULD SAY IS "IMPRACTICAL," TIGERS LOVE.
> - ENTERTAINMENT CENTERS

FEATURE BENEFIT SELLING

A FEATURE IS A FEATURE, BUT THE BENEFIT IS DIFFERENT FOR EACH ANIMAL PERSONALITY.

NOT EVERYONE LIKES THE SAME THING OR THE SAME FEATURE.

> **EXAMPLE**
>
> **OUT OF 100 FEATURES AND ATTRIBUTES, WOULD YOU AGREE THAT OUT OF 2000 HOME BUYERS, MOST EVERYONE PUTS ENERGY-EFFICIENCY, MOLD-PROOF AND FIRE-PROOF AT THE TOP 10%? HOW ABOUT THE TOP 25%?**
>
> IN A RANDOM TEST OF A GROUP OF ACTUAL POTENTIAL BUYERS LOOKING FOR A NEW HOME, ONLY OWLS AND LAMBS HAD THESE THREE VARIABLES IN THE TOP 25%. TIGERS HAD THOSE THREE ITEMS IN THE LOWER 25% AND BULLS HAD THEM IN THE LOWER 50%.

THIS ACTUALLY "SHOCKS" SOME PEOPLE WHO SAY EVERYONE SHOULD BE INTERESTED IN ENERGY EFFICIENCY. YET TIGERS DO NOT PUT ENERGY EFFICIENCY IN THE TOP 75% OF FEATURES AND BENEFITS. OBVIOUSLY NOT EVERYONE LIKES THE SAME THING.

LET'S DO A COUPLE MORE. "WHAT IS THE FEATURE OF A HOME WITH A CEILING HEIGHT OF 20 FEET?" GO AHEAD AND ANSWER THAT. (IT'S KIND OF A TRICK QUESTION.)

THE <u>FEATURE</u> IS THE 20 FT CEILING. THE BENEFIT IS DIFFERENT FOR EACH ANIMAL PERSONALITY.

> **THE FEATURE OF A 20 FT CEILING FOR ANY OF THE ANIMAL PERSONALITIES IS THE 20 FT CEILING.**
>
> FOR THE <u>TIGER</u> THE BENEFIT IS: FUN, EXCITING AND DIFFERENT.
>
> FOR THE <u>BULL</u> THE BENEFIT IS: STRIKING, IMPRESSIVE AND MAKES A STATEMENT.
>
> FOR THE <u>OWL</u> AND <u>LAMB</u> IT IS ACTUALLY AN "ANTI-BENEFIT."
>
> > THE <u>OWL</u> LIKES A HOME THAT IS PRACTICAL, EFFICIENT & FUNCTIONAL. TO THEM, A 20 FT CEILING IS NONE OF THOSE.
>
> > A LAMB LIKES A HOME THAT IS WARM, COZY AND COMFORTABLE.

> # ASSIGNMENT – LIST 20 FEATURES AND THEN THE BENEFITS FOR EACH ANIMAL PERSONALITY FOR <u>EACH</u> OF YOUR HOMES.

WE HAVE 30 YEARS OF RESEARCH ON JUST ABOUT EVERY FEATURE IMAGINABLE IN A HOME AND WHAT EACH ANIMAL PERSONALITY SAYS IS THE VALUE TO THEM AND THEIR PERSONALITY.

IT TRULY IS AN AMAZING SCIENCE!

HERE IS THE MISTAKE THAT SALESPEOPLE CAN RUN INTO.

"I CAN HARDLY WAIT TO SHOW YOU THE MASTER BEDROOM OF THIS HOME. IT IS FUN, EXCITING AND HUGELY SPACIOUS."

YOU SEE WHAT IS COMING. THEY MAY BE PRESENTING TO AN OWL, WHO WILL BE TOTALLY UNIMPRESSED AND **WILL DISCOUNT EVERYTHING ELSE THE SALESPERSON SAYS.** THE OWL MAY SEE THE "HUGELY SPACIOUS" MASTER BEDROOM AS WASTED SPACE.

> DO YOU HAVE FOUR DIFFERENT PRESENTATIONS (DEMONSTRATIONS); ONE FOR EACH PERSONALITY WITH FEATURE/BENEFIT DEMONSTRATIONS DESIGNED FOR EACH PERSONALITY?

> MOST EVERY NATIONAL BUILDER HAS THEIR OWN "UNIQUE-ENERGY EFFICIENCY" PROGRAM THAT THEY ARE SO PROUD OF. (SOME ARE ALMOST ALL THE SAME.) THEY WANT THEIR SALES STAFF TO "TOUT" THEIR "UNIQUE-ENERGY EFFICIENCY" PROGRAM TO ALL BUYERS RIGHT AWAY. OUR RESEARCH INDICATES ONLY ABOUT 25% OF THE ENTIRE POPULATION IS REALLY ENGAGED IN THIS. IT'S ALL IN THE TIMING. I'M NOT DISCOUNTING YOUR "UNIQUE-ENERGY EFFICIENCY" PROGRAM. I'M JUST SAYING YOU MIGHT NOT HAVE EVERYONE'S ATTENTION.

DO YOU HAVE SEPARATE FLOOR PLANS THAT ARE PROTOTYPE:

    BULL HOME?

        OWL HOME?

            LAMB HOME?

                TIGER HOME?

THINGS I AGREE WITH

THINGS I DISAGREE WITH

THINGS I NEED TO WORK ON

ACTION PLAN FOR ME

CHAPTER XIX

> **QUESTION #16:** IT IS OF UTMOST IMPORTANCE TO FIND "COMMON GROUND" WITH THE BUYER AND MAINTAIN THAT COMMON GROUND THROUGHOUT THE SELLING PROCESS.

> # LIE/MYTH #16: IT IS OF UTMOST IMPORTANCE TO FIND COMMON GROUND WITH THE BUYER AND MAINTAIN COMMON GROUND THROUGHOUT THE PRESENTATION.

THE BOTTOM LINE IS THAT THE TWO NON-EMOTIONAL PERSONALITIES, BULLS AND OWLS, DO <u>NOT</u> WANT YOU TO BUILD COMMON GROUND AND RESENT IT IF YOU DO. (50% OF THE POPULATION)

EXAMPLE

A BULL DRIVES INTO A COMMUNITY IN THE SPRING OR SUMMER, AND

> YOU BUILD "COMMON GROUND" WITH THE BULL AND THE OWL BY **NOT TRYING** TO BUILD COMMON GROUND WITH THEM. DOES THAT MAKE SENSE?

HAS GOLF CLUBS SHOWING IN THEIR CAR.

THE SALESPERSON SEES THE GOLF CLUBS AND AFTER MEETING AND GREETING COMMENTS,

SALESPERSON: "I SEE YOU HAVE GOLF CLUBS IN YOUR CAR. ARE YOU GOING TO BE PLAYING TODAY?"

BULL BUYER: "YES, WHAT IS THE PRICE OF THIS HOME?"

SALESPERSON: "OH, WHERE WILL YOU BE PLAYING?"

BULL BUYER: "MEADOWVIEW, AND THE PRICE OF THIS HOME IS?"

> **AGAIN: THE BULL-OWL DOES NOT WANT YOU TO BUILD COMMON GROUND AND YOU BUILD COMMON GROUND BY <u>NOT</u> TRYING TO BUILD COMMON GROUND.**

DOES THIS MAKE SENSE?

THIS FLIES IN THE FACE OF ALMOST EVERYTHING ELSE YOU HAVE HEARD OR READ ABOUT "<u>ALWAYS BUILD COMMON GROUND WITH EVERYONE!</u>" **NOT TRUE!**

THINGS I AGREE WITH

THINGS I DISAGREE WITH

THINGS I NEED TO WORK ON

ACTION PLAN FOR ME

CHAPTER XX

> **QUESTION #17:** MEMORIZING "SCRIPTS," "WORD FOR WORD," AND USING THESE MEMORIZED SCRIPTS VERBATIM ARE EXTREMELY IMPORTANT FOR THE SALESPERSON TO BECOME THE ABSOLUTE BEST. YES/NO

LIE/MYTH #17: MEMORIZING "SCRIPTS" WORD FOR WORD, AND USING THE MEMORIZED SCRIPT WORD FOR WORD, IS EXTREMELY IMPORTANT FOR THE SALESPERSON TO BECOME THE ABSOLUTE BEST.

DURING OUR LAST RECENT RECESSION IN OUR HOME BUILDING INDUSTRY FOLLOWING THE "BOOM" OF '05 AND '06, MANY COMPANIES REVERTED BACK TO THESE INACCURATE MEMORIZED SCRIPTS, WORD FOR WORD, AND SAW THEIR SALES PLUMMET EVEN MORE. THOSE WORD-FOR-WORD,

> **I COULDN'T DISAGREE WITH THIS MORE!**

> TWO REASONS I AM SO OPPOSED ARE #1) IT DOESN'T WORK IF SALESPEOPLE JUST MEMORIZE CLOSES WITHOUT KNOWING WHICH CLOSES <u>WORK</u> AND <u>DON'T WORK</u> WITH DIFFERENT PERSONALITIES, AND #2) SALESPEOPLE BECOME "ROBOTIC" AS A RESULT OF JUST MEMORIZING LISTS OF CLOSES.

> MANY OF THESE LISTS OF CLOSES WERE DEVELOPED IN THE LATE 1950'S AND 1960'S BY J. DOUGLAS EDWARDS', (NOT THE NEWSCASTER) IN "FOUNDATIONS OF MODERN SELLING." HE WAS THE INSPIRATION BEHIND TOMMY HOPKINS. IT MAY HAVE BEEN RIGHT FOR THE 1950'S, 1960'S, AND POSSIBLY EVEN THE 1970'S AND 1980'S, BUT THE MATERIAL IS OUTDATED AND IN MANY CASES JUST PLAIN INACCURATE FOR THIS TIME PERIOD. I RECOMMEND YOU FIND AND READ THE BOOK, BECAUSE IT IS A PART OF OUR HISTORY.

MEMORIZED SCRIPTS MAKE A SALESPERSON NOT THINK AND NOT PAY ATTENTION TO THEIR BUYER (TWO THINGS THAT ARE EXTREMELY IMPORTANT IN BECOMING A MASTER CLOSER).

EARLIER I GAVE AN EXAMPLE UNDER MY "LIE/MYTH #13," ABOUT URGENT CLOSES THAT CAME INDIRECTLY OUT OF J. DOUGLAS EDWARDS FROM THE 1950'S AND WERE LATER ADOPTED BY TOMMY HOPKINS IN HIS BOOK, "MASTER THE ART OF SELLING."

THAT BOOK IS STILL IN PRINT. GET A COPY AND SPECIFICALLY LOOK AT THE CLOSES.

LET ME GIVE JUST TWO EXAMPLES OF CLOSES FROM THOSE WORKS.

1) THE FEEL, FELT, FOUND CLOSE

AND

2) THE "T-BAR"/BEN FRANKLIN CLOSE

EXAMPLE 1

"FEEL, FELT, FOUND"

THIS CLOSE CAN BE USED WHEN A POTENTIAL BUYER SAYS THEY WANT A LOWER PRICE.

SALESPERSON IS SUPPOSED TO SAY, "I CAN APPRECIATE HOW YOU '<u>FEEL</u>,' WE HAVE HAD OTHER BUYERS WHO HAVE '<u>FELT</u>' THAT WAY, AND THEY '<u>FOUND</u>' THAT IF WE LOWERED THE PRICE FOR THEM, IT WOULD HURT THE OVERALL VALUE OF THE ENTIRE COMMUNITY."

CAN YOU SEE WHO THAT COULD "POSSIBLY" APPEAL TO? THE ANSWER IS THE LAMB, BUT HOW DO YOU THINK THE BULL WOULD REACT TO THAT?

BULLS DON'T CARE ABOUT "FEEL, FELT, FOUND" AND RESENT YOU EVEN TALKING LIKE THAT TO THEM. THE BULL SAYS "I DON'T CARE HOW YOU OR OTHERS FEEL OR WHAT YOU FELT OR FOUND. JUST GIVE ME A LOWER PRICE AND QUIT TALKING DOWN TO ME!"

THAT IS AN EXACT QUOTE I HEARD FROM A BULL PROSPECTIVE BUYER AT A COMMUNITY WHERE I OBSERVED THE SALESPERSON USING THE "FEEL, FELT, FOUND" CLOSE ON THE WRONG PERSONALITY.

DON'T INSULT THE INTELLIGENCE OF YOUR BUYER BY USING OUTDATED ROBOTIC CLOSES THAT NEVER WORKED, WITH SOME PERSONALITIES.

> **EXAMPLE #2**

> **THE "T BAR CLOSE" ALSO KNOWN AS THE "BEN FRANKLIN CLOSE"**

AN <u>EXCELLENT</u> CLOSE EVEN TO THIS DAY, BUT WHEN SALESPEOPLE ARE ASKED TO MEMORIZE THIS CLOSE THEY ARE NOT TOLD THAT IT ONLY WORKS ON ABOUT ¼ OF ALL PEOPLE (OWLS).

> **IT IS AN OWL CLOSE, AND WORKS VERY WELL ON OWLS (NO ONE ELSE).**

IN THE AUTO-BIOGRAPHY OF BEN FRANKLIN, BEN FRANKLIN EXPRESSED HOW HE MADE DECISIONS. WHEN HE HAD TO MAKE A DECISION HE SAID HE WOULD WRITE DOWN ALL THE REASONS FOR GOING AHEAD WITH IT IN ONE COLUMN AND ALL THE REASONS FOR NOT GOING AHEAD WITH IT IN ANOTHER COLUMN. IN SOME CASES HE "WEIGHTED" SOME OF THE ANSWERS WITH MORE EMPHASIS. HE WOULD THEN METHODICALLY AND ANALYTICALLY MEASURE THE LOGICAL ANSWERS.

BEN FRANKLIN WAS AN OWL. (OWL WITH BULL TO OWL WITH TIGER, BUT AN OWL.)

> MY POINT IS THAT THIS IS AN OWL CLOSE, TO BE USED ON OWLS ONLY! WITH OTHER PERSONALITIES IT JUST GETS THEM AGGRAVATED.
>
> IF YOU USE THE BEN FRANKLIN CLOSE WITH TIGERS, CAN'T YOU JUST IMAGINE THEM "WONDERING WHAT THEY ARE GOING TO HAVE FOR DINNER," AND NOT PAYING ANY ATTENTION TO THE SALESPERSON?

> **IT JUST INFURIATES BULLS!**

THE "T BAR CLOSE" IS ACTUALLY THE SAME AS THE BEN FRANKLIN CLOSE.

ON THE ONE SIDE (LEFT) LIST ALL THE REASONS FOR GOING AHEAD. ON THE OTHER SIDE (RIGHT) LIST ALL THE REASONS FOR NOT GOING AHEAD WITH IT.

> OWLS OFTEN "T BAR" THEMSELVES! AGAIN, IT IS A GREAT TOOL FOR OWLS, BUT IT WILL BACKFIRE ON YOU WITH ALL THE OTHERS.

YET, WHEN J. DOUGLAS EDWARD, TOMMY HOPKINS AND OTHERS TO THIS DAY TALK ABOUT MEMORIZING THIS AND USING IT THEY NEVER (TO MY KNOWLEDGE) MENTION THE WARNING TO ONLY USE IT WITH THE ANALYTICAL OWL PERSONALITY.

> I HAVE WITNESSED SALES LOST BECAUSE OF THIS MISUSE. DON'T FALL INTO THAT CATEGORY.

SEE MY BOOK ON "KILLER CLOSES FOR DIFFERENT PERSONALITIES™," (2014 RELEASE,) WHERE I TAKE ALL THE CLOSES WE HAVE EVER HEARD OR SEEN AND REDUCE THEM DOWN TO CLOSES AND DEFINITIONS OF WHICH WORKS "BEST" AND "WORST" WITH EACH OF MY ANIMAL PERSONALITIES. AS MENTIONED BEFORE IN THIS BOOK, MY "TENT CARD" WHICH IS AVAILABLE FOR YOUR ASKING, HAS SOME OF THE "KILLER CLOSES™" ON THE BACK OF THE TENT CARD.

"KILLER CLOSES FOR EACH PERSONALITY™" IS THE 3RD DAY SEMINAR IN MY MASTER CLOSER TRILOGY SERIES.

GO AHEAD AND MAKE A LIST OF ALL THE CLOSES YOU KNOW AND USE! WHAT NUMBER DID YOU GET UP TO? GO THROUGH AND MARK WHICH OF THOSE CLOSES WOULD WORK BEST AND WORST FOR EACH ANIMAL PERSONALITY.

CAN YOU NAME 46 DIFFERENT CLOSES?

THINGS I AGREE WITH

THINGS I DISAGREE WITH

THINGS I NEED TO WORK ON

ACTION PLAN FOR ME

CHAPTER XXI

> **QUESTION #18:** A "1 IN 10" CLOSING RATIO (10%) IS THE ULTIMATE CLOSING RATIO FOR WHICH A SALESPERSON SHOULD STRIVE. YES/NO

> # LIE/MYTH #18: A "1 IN 10" CLOSING RATIO, 10%, IS THE ULTIMATE CLOSING RATIO FOR WHICH A SALESPERSON SHOULD BE STRIVING.

YOU NOW KNOW THE ANSWER TO THIS FROM PREVIOUS DISCUSSIONS IN THIS BOOK.

A 1 IN 10 CLOSING RATIO (10%) IS EXCELLENT, BUT IT IS NOT THE MASTER CLOSER LEVEL.

AGAIN:

IF A SALESPERSON IS AT THIS "EXCELLENT" LEVEL 1 IN 10, WHAT DOES THAT MEAN? IT MEANS FOR EVERY 10 PEOPLE THEY SEE (WHETHER QUALIFIED OR NOT) THEY ARE LOSING 9 OUT OF EVERY 10. NOW OF COURSE SOME OF THESE "POTENTIAL BUYERS" ARE NOT REALLY POTENTIAL. SOME ARE NOT READY, SOME ARE NOT WILLING AND SOME ARE NOT ABLE (CAN'T EVEN AFFORD A GOOD PEN AND PENCIL SET).

CLOSING RATIOS ARE BASED ON <u>TOTAL</u> TRAFFIC, NOT JUST QUALIFIED TRAFFIC. COUNT <u>ALL</u> BUYING UNITS.

> # MY QUESTION TO YOU IS, IF YOU ARE 1 IN 10 (EXCELLENT) IS THERE SOMETHING/ANYTHING YOU COULD SAY OR DO TO GET JUST 1 OF THOSE 9 THAT GOT AWAY?

IS THERE ANYTHING FROM THE PREVIOUS 17 LIES/MYTHS THAT YOU COULD APPLY TO GET JUST 1 OF THOSE 9 THAT GOT AWAY?

IF SO, YOU WOULD BE AT A 2 IN 10 OR A 1 IN 5 AND YOU WOULD HAVE LITERALLY <u>DOUBLED</u> YOUR SALES AND WOULD BECOME A MASTER CLOSER (1 IN 5). I MENTION THIS SEVERAL TIMES, BECAUSE IT IS SO IMPORTANT.

YOUR THOUGHTS?

GO BACK THROUGH THE PREVIOUS 17 LIES/MYTHS AND CHECK THE ONES THAT YOU THINK COULD SPECIFICALLY MAKE THE DIFFERENCE IN YOU GETTING 1 OF THOSE 9 THAT GOT AWAY.

IF A SALESPERSON IS "AVERAGE" (1 IN 20), THEY WILL GET 5 SALES FOR EVERY 100 TRAFFIC UNITS, WHERE A MASTER CLOSER WILL GET 20 SALES OUT OF THAT SAME 100 TRAFFIC UNITS.

4 TIMES AS MUCH/EARNING 4 TIMES AS MUCH

☆ *ANOTHER WAY OF LOOKING AT IT IS, A BUILDER WOULD BE LOSING 15 POTENTIAL SALES, WITH THAT AVERAGE SALESPERSON, WITH THE SAME 100 TRAFFIC UNITS!*

OFTENTIMES A BUILDER HAS A CHOICE OF SPENDING $100,000+ MORE ON MARKETING TO GET MORE TRAFFIC, WHEN REALLY WHAT THEY NEED TO BE CONCENTRATING ON IS GETTING BETTER CLOSING RATIOS FROM ALL THEIR SALESPEOPLE.

THINGS I AGREE WITH

THINGS I DISAGREE WITH

THINGS I NEED TO WORK ON

ACTION PLAN FOR ME

CHAPTER XXII

> **QUESTION #19:** IT IS BEST TO ALWAYS HAVE THE BUILDER PRICE THE HOME HIGHER THAN WHAT THE BUILDER WOULD SELL IT, SO YOU CAN NEGOTIATE THE PRICE LOWER. YES/NO

> # LIE/MYTH #19: IT IS BEST TO ALWAYS HAVE THE PRICE OF THE HOME HIGHER THAN WHAT THE BUILDER WOULD SELL IT, SO YOU CAN NEGOTIATE THE PRICE LOWER.

THIS IS A VERY CONTROVERSIAL TOPIC WITH BUILDERS, SALES MANAGERS AND SALESPEOPLE IN THIS DAY AND AGE.

THOSE OF YOU WHO HAVE BEEN AROUND A LONG TIME KNOW THAT OUR INDUSTRY NEVER NEGOTIATED UP UNTIL ABOUT 2007 OR 2008. WE DIDN'T HAVE TO! NEGOTIATING WAS FOR "USED HOMES"/"EXISTING HOMES" NOT FOR OUR NEW HOME INDUSTRY.

THEN ALONG CAME THE RECESSION AND OUR INDUSTRY STARTED NEGOTIATING LIKE CRAZY.

> ## I'M SUGGESTING THAT WE COMPLETELY STOP NEGOTIATING AGAIN, AS AN ENTIRE INDUSTRY.

PLEASE HAVE A MEETING WITH YOUR ENTIRE COMPANY, AND WITH YOUR TOP MANAGEMENT, ABOUT THIS DISCUSSION.

WHEN THE LAST RECESSION STARTED IN APPROXIMATELY 2007 AND 2008 (THE TIMING VARIED IN DIFFERENT GEOGRAPHICAL LOCATIONS), MANY BUILDERS HAD TO LITERALLY TAKE A LOSS IN SOME OF THEIR INVENTORY HOMES, TO BE ABLE TO SELL THEM.

I UNDERSTAND.

THIS IS WHAT I'M SUGGESTING NOW! <u>DO NOT NEGOTIATE AT ALL!</u> DECIDE IN ADVANCE WHAT THE LOWEST PRICE IS THAT YOUR COMPANY WOULD TAKE FOR THE HOME, ALLOWING THE PROFIT THEY WANT AS A NET NET FIGURE, AND THEN STICK WITH THAT NUMBER.

I GET AGGRAVATED WHEN SOME OF MY BUILDERS RAISE THE PRICE OF THE HOME JUST TO LOWER IT (HOPING AND WISHING FOR THAT HIGHER PRICE).

THIS IS A MYTH, THAT A BUYER <u>HAS TO</u> FEEL GOOD ABOUT NEGOTIATING THE PRICE DOWN AND IF THEY DON'T GET A BETTER PRICE THAN THE "STICKER PRICE," THEY WON'T BUY. NOT TRUE!

LET'S TAKE A LOOK AT HOW EACH OF MY ANIMAL PERSONALITIES REACTS TO NEGOTIATING.

BULLS AND "CULTURAL BUYERS"

BULLS, WHO ARE SOME OF THE TOUGHEST NEGOTIATORS ALONG WITH OWLS, WILL BUY EVEN IF YOU DON'T LOWER THE PRICE. TREAT "CULTURAL BUYERS," (WHO ARE BY THEIR CULTURE FORCED TO FEEL AS THEY HAVE TO NEGOTIATE), AS BULLS.

> **THE BULLS JUST HAVE TO BE TOLD AND BELIEVE THAT <u>NO ONE ELSE</u> WILL OR CAN GET A BETTER PRICE THAN THEM.**

SALESPERSON TO THE BULL IN THE END OF THE GAME OF SELLING, "ON THIS $525,000 YOU ARE ASKING US TO SELL IT TO YOU FOR $500,000." THE ANSWER IS, "NO." "AS I MENTIONED EARLIER, <u>WE DO NOT NEGOTIATE.</u> I HOPE YOU BELIEVE THAT, BECAUSE IT IS TRUE. NO ONE ELSE WILL BE ABLE TO BUY THIS HOME FOR LESS THAN $525,000." (YOU CAN ONLY SAY THIS IF EVERYONE ON THE MANAGEMENT TEAM AGREES JUST LIKE WE USE TO BEFORE THIS LAST RECESSION.)

> **IT HAS TO BE COMPETITIVELY PRICED, WITH YOUR DESIRED PROFIT. THEN DON'T NEGOTIATE!**

YOU COULD GO ON TO SAY, "YOU ARE WANTING $25,000 LESS THAN THE PRICE FOR WHICH WE WILL SELL IT, AND THE ANSWER AGAIN IS NO. IF YOU WANTED TO PAY $10,000 OR $5,000 LESS, THE ANSWER WOULD STILL BE "NO!" AGAIN IF YOU LIKE THIS HOME BUT DON'T BELIEVE THIS, YOU WILL BUY FROM SOMEONE ELSE AND POSSIBLY BUY

A HOME THAT YOU DON'T LIKE AS MUCH. I HOPE YOU DON'T, BUT THIS IS THE LOWEST PRICE THAT ANYONE WILL BE ABLE TO BUY IT."

> YOU COULD GO ON TO SAY, "WHAT WE HAVE DONE IS NEGOTIATE FOR YOU. SOME JEWELRY STORES AND SOME BUILDERS RAISE THEIR PRICES ONLY TO LOWER THEM SO THE BUYER THINKS THEY ARE GETTING A GOOD DEAL. WE HAVE ALREADY NEGOTIATED FOR YOU. THIS IS OUR LOWEST PRICE."

YOUR THOUGHTS?

OBVIOUSLY ALL THAT DIALOGUE WOULD BE TOO LONG FOR A BULL AND OF COURSE I'M NOT ASKING YOU TO MEMORIZE IT. THIS WOULD BE AGAINST MY PRINCIPLES. GO THROUGH AND HIGHLIGHT WHAT ASPECTS OF THE DIALOGUE WOULD WORK FOR YOU.

YOU HAVE TO HAVE THE COOPERATION OF YOUR BUILDER AND MANAGER ON THIS, SO YOU ARE ALL "SINGING OUT OF THE SAME HYMNAL."

NEVER, NEVER SAY TO ANY POTENTIAL BUYER, "MAKE ME AN OFFER" OR "WHAT DO YOU HAVE IN MIND." NEVER!

THE ABOVE PHRASES ARE FOR "USED HOMES"/"EXISTING HOMES," **NOT** FOR NEW HOME SALES.

I'M SUGGESTING THAT FOR ALL MY ANIMAL PERSONALITIES YOU START OFF BY SAYING "NO," BUT IT'S ALL IN HOW YOU DELIVER THE "NO."

IT'S ALL IN THE PRESENTATION.

BULLS WANT TO MAKE SURE THAT NO ONE ELSE CAN, OR IS GOING TO, GET A BETTER PRICE. THEY NEGOTIATE "HARD, FAST AND OFTEN."

OWLS NEGOTIATE WITH LOGIC AND THEY ARE JUST AS TOUGH AS BULLS (OWLS USE LOGIC).

OWL SAYS, "THE BUILDER DOWN THE STREET IS OFFERING BASICALLY THIS SAME HOUSE WITH MORE SQUARE FOOTAGE FOR A LOWER PRICE." HOW DO YOU EXPLAIN THAT?

SALESPERSON REPLIES, "IF IT IS SUCH A BETTER HOME AND AT A BETTER PRICE, WHY DIDN'T YOU BUY IT?"

OWL BUYER SAYS, "I DIDN'T SAY IT WAS A BETTER HOME, JUST LARGER (MORE SQUARE FOOTAGE) AND A LOWER PRICE."

SALESPERSON REPLIES, "LET'S SIT DOWN AND TAKE A LOOK AT BOTH HOMES AND MAKE SURE WE ARE COMPARING APPLES TO APPLES AND ORANGES TO ORANGES. ARE YOU FAMILIAR WITH WHAT IS SOMETIMES CALLED, 'THE T-BAR CLOSE OR BEN FRANKLIN CLOSE?'"

OWL BUYER SAYS, "OF COURSE."

SALESPERSON, "WELL, LET'S DO THAT IN WRITING WITH BOTH HOMES AND LOOK AT THE VALUE OF EACH."

YOUR THOUGHTS?

THE TWO BEST NEGOTIATORS ARE BULLS AND OWLS (NOT NECESSARILY IN THAT ORDER.)

THE TWO WORST NEGOTIATORS ARE LAMBS AND TIGERS, BUT THEY STILL BOTH "ATTEMPT" TO NEGOTIATE.

LAMBS

LAMB SAYS, "I HAVE BEEN TOLD BY FRIENDS AND RELATIVES NOT TO ACCEPT YOUR ORIGINAL PRICE, SO PLEASE TELL ME IF I CAN GET A BETTER PRICE THAN THIS."

SALESPERSON "NO, I REALLY WOULD LOVE TO DO THAT FOR YOU BUT I REALLY CANNOT LOWER THE PRICE AT ALL. IF I COULD, I WOULD. AS I MENTIONED, THERE IS THIS PUBLICIZED SPECIAL GOING ON UNTIL THE END OF THE THIS MONTH AND THAT IS TRULY THE BEST I CAN DO FOR YOU. ARE YOU READY TO PROCEED?"

> # IT'S THE SAME ANSWER, BUT "IT'S ALL IN THE PRESENTATION!" CHARLES J. CLARKE III

TIGERS

> # TIGERS WILL FAKE NEGOTIATION, JUST FOR THE FUN OF THE FAKE! TIGERS FAKE A LOT OF THINGS, JUST FOR THE FUN OF IT.

TIGER SAYS WHEN BUYING A RED CORVETTE, "I AM NOT GOING TO PAY STICKER PRICE. NOT GOING TO DO IT!"

CAR SALESMAN, "WHY DON'T YOU TAKE IT FOR A DRIVE DOWN THAT ROAD OVER THERE, PUNCH IT OUT. FIRST LET'S PUT THE TOP DOWN."

WHEN THE TIGER COMES BACK FROM THE DRIVE, SALESPERSON SAYS "HOW DID IT FEEL? HOW DID THE NEW CAR SMELL? HOW DID IT DRIVE? READY TO GO AHEAD WITH THIS TODAY?"

"SURE." (THE TIGER "FORGOT" ABOUT THE NEGOTIATING.) (THE TRICK NOW IS TO GET THEM FINANCED.)

TIGERS ARE THE WORST NEGOTIATORS BECAUSE THEY GET ALL CAUGHT UP IN THE EMOTIONS OF THE PURCHASES. (OWLS DON'T.)

GET THE TIGER TO "IMAGINE" HOW THEY ARE GOING TO ENTERTAIN IN THEIR NEW HOME. "IMAGINE HOW MUCH YOU ARE GOING TO ENJOY THIS HOME."

> TOUGH THING ABOUT SELLING HOMES TO TIGERS IS GETTING THEM QUALIFIED FOR A MORTGAGE. THAT'S A DISCUSSION FOR A WHOLE OTHER TOPIC.

WHILE WE ARE STILL ON PRICING, WHAT'S WITH SOME COMPANIES STILL HAVING HOMES PRICED $199,950 OR $999,950?

FIRST OF ALL TIGERS THINK IT'S JUST TOO MANY NUMBERS AND BULLS THEY THINK YOU ARE TRYING TO TRICK THEM INTO THINKING THAT IT IS REALLY NOT A $200,000 HOME OR A MILLION DOLLAR HOME.

WHEN A COUPLE IS BUYING A MILLION DOLLAR HOME DO THEY TELL THEIR FRIENDS, "I BOUGHT THE HOME FOR $999,950?" NO! THEY SAY, "WE BOUGHT A MILLION DOLLAR HOME."

WE'RE NOT SELLING SHIRTS AT $99 IN ORDER TO **NOT** HAVE IT LOOK LIKE A $100.

A SIMILAR SUBJECT IS ABOUT OWL BUILDERS WHO STILL INSIST ON CALLING THEIR HOMES BY NUMBER AND NOT NAMES. "THIS IS THE 1950" OR "THE 2410" (REFERRING TO SQUARE FOOTAGE). LAMBS AND TIGERS FIND THAT VERY NON-EMOTIONAL AND "COLD."

YOUR THOUGHTS?

THINGS I AGREE WITH

THINGS I DISAGREE WITH

THINGS I NEED TO WORK ON

ACTION PLAN FOR ME

CHAPTER XXIII

> **QUESTION #20:** THE MOST IMPORTANT ACCOMPLISHMENT A NEW HOME SALES CONSULTANT CAN ACCOMPLISH ON THE FIRST VISIT, IS TO GIVE THE BEST PRESENTATION POSSIBLE TO GET THE BUYER EXCITED ENOUGH TO COME BACK. YES/NO

> # LIE/MYTH #20: THE MOST IMPORTANT ACCOMPLISHMENT A NEW HOME SALES CONSULTANT CAN ACCOMPLISH THE FIRST VISIT IS TO GIVE THE BEST PRESENTATION POSSIBLE TO GET THE BUYER EXCITED ENOUGH TO COME BACK.

WE'VE PRETTY MUCH COVERED THAT THE MOST IMPORTANT TASK THAT A SALESPERSON CAN REALLY ACCOMPLISH IS TO <u>CLOSE</u> THEM THAT VERY FIRST DAY. AT LEAST 33% (⅓ TO ½) OF YOUR SALES COULD BE AND SHOULD BE DONE THE FIRST DAY. HALF OF THE BUYERS (TIGERS AND BULLS) SAY THAT IS THEIR PREFERENCE. SO CLOSE THEM THE WAY <u>THEY</u> WANT TO BE CLOSED.

> **IF THEY LEAVE WITHOUT A SIGNED CONTRACT ALWAYS HAVE A SCHEDULED "NEXT APPOINTMENT" OR AT LEAST A SCHEDULED "TENTATIVE APPOINTMENT."**

> *THE TRUTH IS THAT ABOUT 2/3'S OF YOUR BUYERS TO 1/2 WILL NOT BUY THE FIRST DAY SO YOU BETTER MAKE SURE YOUR "FOLLOW UP" IS 100% ON THE MONEY.*

I MENTIONED EARLIER THAT THE AVERAGE "BEEN BACK" RATIO IS ABOUT 8% TO 10%. WITH REALLY GREAT "FOLLOW UP" YOU CAN GET THAT UP TO 16% TO 20%.

I HAVE WORKED WITH SOME SALESPEOPLE WHO HAVE SAID (BEFORE WE REALLY STARTED WORKING TOGETHER) THAT THEIR GOAL WAS TO <u>NOT</u> GET THE APPOINTMENT WHILE THE POTENTIAL BUYER WAS STILL THERE BUT TO CALL THEM THE NEXT DAY AND SET THE APPOINTMENT THEN ON THE PHONE.

> **SET THE APPOINTMENT WHILE THEY ARE STILL THERE.**

THINGS I AGREE WITH

THINGS I DISAGREE WITH

THINGS I NEED TO WORK ON

ACTION PLAN FOR ME

PART 3

CHAPTER	LIE/MYTH	PAGES
XXIV	% HAVING BEEN TO YOUR WEBSITE	117
XXV	BUYING ON EMOTION AND JUSTIFYING WITH LOGIC	119
XXVI	SELLING TO ACTIVE ADULTS	121
XXVII	SELLING RESORT COMMUNITIES	125
XXVIII	SELLING CUSTOM HOMES	127
XXIX	100+ OBJECTIONS	131
XXX	SELLING HIGH END HOMES	139
XXXI	ASKING QUESTIONS STANDING UP	141
XXXII	BRINGING OUT THE CONTRACT AFTER THEY HAVE SAID "NO"	149
XXXIII	FLAWED PRODUCT	155
XXXIV	CONCLUSION	157
XXXV	SUMMARY OF "30 MYTHS" IN SELLING NEW HOMES	159

CHAPTER XXIV

QUESTION #21: 92% OF ALL POTENTIAL BUYERS HAVE ALREADY GONE TO YOUR WEBSITE BEFORE VISITING YOU. YES/NO

LIE/MYTH #21: 92% OF ALL POTENTIAL BUYERS HAVE GONE TO YOUR WEBSITE.

I JUST HEARD THIS LIE/MYTH AT A RECENT CONVENTION! WHERE DID THEY COME UP WITH THAT? WHAT SAMPLE DID THEY USE? WHERE WAS IT?

AT THE SAME CONVENTION I HEARD ANOTHER SPEAKER SAY, "83% OF YOUR BUYERS HAVE ALREADY BEEN TO YOUR WEBSITE BEFORE THEY CAME IN."

(SURPRISE. BOTH OF THESE HAPPENED TO HAVE WEBSITE DESIGN BUSINESSES.)

HERE'S THE TRUTH. WE REALLY DON'T KNOW UNLESS WE ASK.

SOME BUILDERS AND SOME REGIONS REPORT THAT THE NUMBER IS LESS THAN 50% THAT GO TO THEIR WEBSITE.

A LOT OF BUILDER REPRESENTATIVES STILL <u>DON'T</u> ASK THE QUESTION OF EVERYONE, "HAVE YOU BEEN TO OUR WEBSITE? DID YOU FIND A HOME YOU LIKED THE BEST? WHICH ONE?"

TIGERS HAVE A HIGH PROBABILITY OF NOT HAVING GONE TO THE WEBSITE FIRST. THEY JUST GO IN. BULLS ALSO WILL DO THIS.

EVERYONE SHOULD BE ASKING THOSE TWO QUESTIONS 100% OF THE TIME, IN THE BEGINNING UNDER QUALIFYING FOR WILLING. IT WILL SAVE YOU A LOT OF TIME NOT TALKING ABOUT WHAT THEY DON'T HAVE AN INTEREST IN.

DON'T ASSUME ANYTHING ABOUT THEM HAVING ALREADY BEEN TO YOUR WEBSITE! ASK!

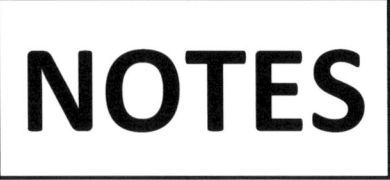

THINGS I AGREE WITH

THINGS I DISAGREE WITH

THINGS I NEED TO WORK ON

ACTION PLAN FOR ME

CHAPTER XXV

> **QUESTION #22:** ALL BUYERS BUY WITH EMOTION AND JUSTIFY IT WITH LOGIC. YES/NO

LIE/MYTH #22: ALL BUYERS BUY WITH EMOTION AND JUSTIFY IT WITH LOGIC.

YOU SEE THE TREND HERE. THIS MYTH HAS NEVER MADE SENSE TO ME, BUT IT CERTAINLY DOES GET PERPETUATED.

TIGERS BUY WITH EMOTION AND JUSTIFY IT WITH EMOTION.

OWLS BUY WITH LOGIC AND JUSTIFY IT WITH LOGIC.

DO YOU BELIEVE THAT? I KNOW THAT TO BE TRUE!

EXAMPLE OF A LAND DEAL (100 ACRES) IN PHOENIX

BACK WHEN I WAS WITH TODAY'S AMERICAN BUILDER, WE WERE TRYING TO GET A PARTICULAR BUILDER INTO A FRANCHISE. HE SAID HE FIRST NEEDED TO SECURE THIS 100 ACRES. WE ASKED IF WE COULD DRIVE AROUND THE PERIMETER AND POSSIBLY SOME OF THE INTERIOR OF THE PROPERTY, IN THE JEEP.

HE SAID HE DID NOT WANT TO DO THAT, BECAUSE HE HAD ALREADY SEEN THE AERIAL MAPS OF THE TERRAIN, THE COMPARABLES AND FINANCIALS, AND HE DID NOT WANT TO TOUR THE PROPERTY.

*HE SAID HE DID NOT WANT TO GET **"EMOTIONALLY INVOLVED!"***

IT WAS ONLY ABOUT THE NUMBERS TO HIM AND HE SAID HE ALWAYS GUARDED AGAINST GETTING EMOTIONALLY INVOLVED WHEN BUYING ANYTHING, EVEN HIS OWN HOME. THIS IS NOT UNUSUAL. ABOUT 50% OF THE POPULATION (OWLS AND BULLS) SAY THEY DO NOT BUY ON EMOTION AND FIND IT VERY AGGRAVATING WHEN A SALESPERSON TRIES TO GET THEM TO DO SO.

THINGS I AGREE WITH

THINGS I DISAGREE WITH

THINGS I NEED TO WORK ON

ACTION PLAN FOR ME

CHAPTER XXVI

> **QUESTION #23:** IN SELLING TO ACTIVE ADULT BUYERS (50 YEARS+) THEY REALLY NEED TO BE TREATED DIFFERENTLY AND CERTAINLY WOULD NOT BUY THE FIRST DAY. YES/NO

> **LIE/MYTH #23: IN SELLING TO ACTIVE ADULTS (50+) THEY REALLY NEED TO BE SOLD AND TREATED DIFFERENTLY AND CERTAINLY WOULDN'T BUY THE FIRST DAY.**

WHO MADE THAT MYTH UP?

YES THE <u>PRODUCT</u> HAS TO BE DIFFERENT, BUT I'M SUGGESTING WHY WOULD YOU SELL TO THEM ANY DIFFERENTLY?

> **YOUNG BULLS, OWLS, LAMBS OR TIGERS® GROW UP TO BE OLDER BULLS, OWLS, LAMBS AND TIGERS® (BUYERS WITH THE SAME ATTRIBUTES).**

60 YEAR OLD TIGERS AND BULLS SAY THEY <u>WOULD</u> BUY THE FIRST DAY, AND WOULD PREFER TO DO SO.

> **EXAMPLE**
>
> DEL WEBB COMMUNITY IN PHOENIX BEFORE IT WAS PART OF PULTE:

BACK A NUMBER OF YEARS AGO (MAYBE 20 YEARS AGO) MY FRIEND SUE CAMERA, WHO WAS AN EXECUTIVE VICE PRESIDENT WITH THEIR SUN CITY COMMUNITIES, BROUGHT ME IN TO HELP IN CONSULTING AND SEMINARS. UP UNTIL THAT TIME THEY HAD NO SALES DONE THE FIRST DAY.

> AFTER APPROXIMATELY 6 MONTHS OF MY COMING IN SEVERAL DAYS EACH MONTH, WE GOT THE NUMBER OF SALES THAT WERE DONE THE "FIRST DAY," TO OVER 35% AND THE TOTAL NUMBER OF SALES MORE THAN DOUBLED EACH MONTH.

> THIS WAS WITH 50+ BUYERS.

> POINT:
>
> IN ACTIVE ADULT COMMUNITIES, IF WE EXPECT THEM NOT TO BUY THE FIRST DAY, THEY WON'T.

> WHEN I START TO WORK WITH ACTIVE ADULT COMMUNITIES (50+) IT'S ALWAYS LIKE "DÉJÀ VU" ALL OVER AGAIN, WITH THE SAME MYTH.

STOP IT!

AGAIN, THIS WAS APPROXIMATELY 20 YEARS AGO, BUT WE REPEAT THOSE SIMILAR STATISTICS WITH VARIOUS 50+ COMMUNITIES, ALL ACROSS AMERICA.

ALSO, WHAT IS THE BIG DEAL ABOUT OVER-EMPHASIZING "COUNSELING" FOR THE 50+ BUYER? MANY 50+ BUYERS REPORT RESENTING THIS.

YOUR THOUGHTS?

THINGS I AGREE WITH

THINGS I DISAGREE WITH

THINGS I NEED TO WORK ON

ACTION PLAN FOR ME

CHAPTER XXVII

> **QUESTION #24:** SELLING RESORT COMMUNITIES IS VERY DIFFERENT FROM SELLING NON-RESORT COMMUNITIES. YES/NO

LIE/MYTH #24: SELLING RESORT COMMUNITIES AND GOLF COURSE COMMUNITIES IS VERY DIFFERENT FROM SELLING NON-RESORT COMMUNITIES.

BELIEVE THAT AND YOU WILL SELL LESS.

YOU GET THE POINT!

> THE COMMUNITY AND AMENITIES ARE DIFFERENT BUT THE "MASTER CLOSER SELLING SKILL SET" IS THE SAME.

LOTS OF RESORT COMMUNITIES AND GOLF COURSE COMMUNITIES THAT WE WORK WITH ARE SO PROUD OF ALL THEIR AMENITIES, THAT THEY WANT THEIR SALES PEOPLE TO TAKE PROSPECTIVE BUYERS ON A SEVERAL HOUR TOUR SHOWING THEM <u>ALL</u> THE AMENITIES.

FOLLOW MY GUIDELINES FROM MY CHAPTER ON SITTING THEM DOWN FIRST IN CHAPTER #31.

> BULLS DON'T WANT TO SEE EVERYTHING. THEY JUST CAME IN TO BUY

> OFTEN TIME WE GO "PAST THE CLOSE" AND DESTROY THE SALE.

> ASK THEM HOW THEY WANT TO PROCEED.

YOUR THOUGHTS?

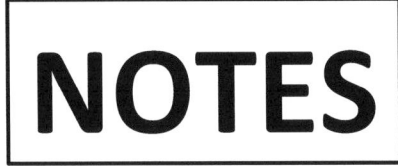

THINGS I AGREE WITH

THINGS I DISAGREE WITH

THINGS I NEED TO WORK ON

ACTION PLAN FOR ME

CHAPTER XXVIII

> **QUESTION #25:** SELLING CUSTOM HOMES "<u>ON THEIR LOT</u>" IS VERY DIFFERENT, AND IF POTENTIAL BUYERS DON'T ALREADY HAVE THEIR OWN LOT (LAND) IN PLACE, THEY CERTAINLY WOULD NOT PURCHASE THE FIRST DAY. YES/NO

> **LIE/MYTH #25: SELLING CUSTOM HOMES "<u>ON THEIR LOT</u>" IS VERY DIFFERENT, AND IF POTENTIAL BUYERS DON'T ALREADY HAVE THEIR OWN LOT (LAND) IN PLACE, THEY CERTAINLY WOULD NOT PURCHASE THE FIRST DAY.**

IT'S REALLY INTERESTING TO ME HOW SOME OF THESE MYTHS GET STARTED AND PERPETUATED.

I USE TO LIVE IN TAMPA, FLORIDA, FOR ABOUT 15 YEARS. THERE WAS AN "ON YOUR LOT" VERY, VERY LARGE NATIONAL COMPANY NAMED

> JIM WALTER HOMES - NO LONGER IN EXISTENCE

THEIR MAIN PREMISE WAS WHEN A POTENTIAL BUYER CAME INTO ONE OF THEIR MULTI-NATIONAL SITES ALL OVER THE UNITED STATES, THE SALESPERSON WOULD SAY, "HELLO! DO YOU HAVE YOUR OWN LAND?" IF THE ANSWER WAS, "NO," THEY REALLY WEREN'T SUPPOSED TO, AND DID NOT "GIVE THEM THE TIME OF DAY" AFTER THAT.

TRUE/TRUE!

WE MYSTERY SHOPPED JIM WALTER HOMES AT OUR OWN EXPENSE.

WE SHOWED THE NATIONAL MANAGEMENT TEAM THE RESULTS OF OUR MYSTERY SHOPS IN ORDER TO TRY TO GET THEIR BUSINESS, IN CHANGING THEIR WAYS! MANAGEMENT'S REACTION TO THAT WAS, "THAT'S THE WAY WE WANT IT. IF THE POTENTIAL BUYERS DON'T HAVE THEIR OWN LAND, THEY ARE NOT OUR CUSTOMERS."

THEY ARE OUT OF BUSINESS! CLOSED!

LET ME SHOW YOU A CONTRAST TO THAT.

> **SCHUMACHER HOMES IS THE LARGEST AND ARGUABLY THE MOST SUCCESSFUL CUSTOM HOME BUILDER (ON YOUR LOT) IN THE UNITED STATES.**

THEY ARE HOME-BASED OUT OF CANTON, OHIO, AND BUILD IN 15 STATES (AND ARE CONSTANTLY EXPANDING).

I USED TO BE THEIR SALES MANAGER IN 2008 FOR THE ENTIRE CAROLINA DIVISION (ALL 9 CITIES). I STILL CONSULT AND GIVE SEMINARS FOR THEM AND WITH THEM ON A REGULAR BASIS.

> **POINT:**
>
> **SOME OF THEIR SALESPEOPLE HAVE A RECORD OF SELLING APPROXIMATELY ⅓+ OF ALL THEIR SALES THE FIRST DAY AND SOME OF THEIR SALESPEOPLE HAVE ⅓+ OF THEIR SALES DONE WITHOUT THE BUYER HAVING THE LAND. IT'S BECAUSE THEY THINK DIFFERENTLY AND HAVE ELIMINATED LIES & MYTHS IN SELLING.**

WE CAN WRITE THIS, "SUBJECT TO YOUR OBTAINING THE LAND WITHIN A TWO WEEK PERIOD OF TIME. IF YOU DON'T HAVE IT BY THEN, WE CAN POSSIBLY EXTEND THE TIME PERIOD."

> **IT'S A DIFFERENT "MIND-SET."**

WHAT IS YOUR "MIND-SET?"

IS YOUR "MIND-SET" ALTERING, AS YOU READ THIS BOOK?

THINGS I AGREE WITH

THINGS I DISAGREE WITH

THINGS I NEED TO WORK ON

ACTION PLAN FOR ME

CHAPTER XXIX

> **QUESTION #26:** THERE COULD BE LITERALLY 100 OBJECTIONS TO WHY A BUYER DOESN'T BUY ONE OF MY HOMES. YES/NO

> # LIE/MYTH #26: THERE ARE LITERALLY OVER 100+ OBJECTIONS TO WHY A POTENTIAL BUYER MIGHT NOT BUY ONE OF OUR HOMES.

IF YOU BELIEVE THIS YOU HAVE JUST COMPLICATED YOUR SELLING LIFE, WAY BEYOND WHAT YOU NEED TO DO.

> ## "THERE ARE ONLY SEVEN OBJECTIONS IN SELLING NEW HOMES™."
>
> **CHARLES CLARKE III**

> ## "ALL OBJECTIONS IN SELLING NEW HOMES CAN BE BROKEN DOWN TO ONLY 7 OBJECTIONS."
>
> **CHARLES CLARKE III**

IF YOU ARE AN ON-YOUR-LOT BUILDER, THERE ARE POSSIBLY EIGHT OBJECTIONS.

THE 8TH ONE BEING, "I DON'T HAVE MY OWN LAND." YET REALISTICALLY YOU COULD COMBINE #8 INTO #4, "I NEED TO TAKE CARE OF SOMETHING ELSE FIRST."

TAKE A MINUTE AND START LISTING 20+ OBJECTIONS OR SOMETHING THAT BLOCKS SOMEONE FROM BUYING YOUR NEW HOME TODAY.

1.
2.
3.
4.
5.
6.
7.
8.
9.
10.
11.
12.
13.
14.
15.
16.
17.
18.
19.
20.

MORE:

LET'S LOOK AT SOME POSSIBLE OBJECTIONS WE HAVE HEARD. AFTER YOU HAVE READ THIS CHAPTER PUT EACH OF THESE 36 OBJECTIONS PLUS YOUR ADDITIONAL ONES, INTO THE CATEGORIES OF THE "ONLY" 7 OBJECTIONS. ALL THESE AND OTHERS FALL INTO THE "7" CATEGORIES.

1)   WE JUST STARTED LOOKING.

2)   WE DON'T REALLY KNOW WHAT WE WANT.

3)   I DON'T HAVE A JOB YET.

4)   I'M HERE IN THIS CITY TO INTERVIEW FOR A JOB.

5)   MY DAUGHTER IS GETTING MARRIED IN SIX MONTHS, SO WE AREN'T GOING TO DO ANYTHING UNTIL THEN.

6)   YOU'RE TOO CLOSE TO THE RAILROAD TRACKS.

7)   YOU'RE ON A LANDFILL.

8)   THAT PIG FARM IS TOO CLOSE.

9)   YOUR COMMUNITY IS TOO FAR AWAY.

10) IT'S TOO CLOSE TO TOWN.

11) YOU ARE TOO FAR FROM THE AIRPORT.

12) YOU ARE TOO CLOSE TO THE AIRPORT.

13) YOUR SITES ARE TOO LARGE (TOO MUCH TO MOW).

14) YOU SITES ARE TOO SMALL; TOO CLOSE TOGETHER.

15) YOU DON'T HAVE ENOUGH AMENITIES.

16) YOU HAVE TOO MANY AMENITIES (WE DON'T SWIM AND DON'T WANT TO PAY FOR SOMEONE ELSE TO SWIM).

17) YOU DON'T MAKE ANY CHANGES.

18) YOU DON'T NEGOTIATE.

19) YOUR PRICE IS TOO HIGH.

20) WE ARE NOT IN YOUR PRICE RANGE.

21) WE DON'T HAVE ENOUGH MONEY FOR THE DOWN PAYMENT.

22) WE DON'T HAVE ENOUGH MONEY FOR THE MONTHLY PAYMENT.

23) WE DON'T HAVE GOOD ENOUGH CREDIT.

24) WE DON'T LIKE YOUR HOME OWNER'S DUES.

25) WE DON'T LIKE YOUR FLOOR PLANS.

26) WE DON'T LIKE YOUR CONSTRUCTION.

27) YOUR SECONDARY BEDROOMS ARE TOO SMALL.

28) YOUR MASTER BEDROOMS (OWNERS RETREAT) IS TOO LARGE (WE DON'T NEED THAT MUCH ROOM).

29) WE NEED A 1-STORY HOME AND YOU DON'T HAVE IT.

30) WE NEED A 2-STORY HOME AND YOU DON'T HAVE IT.

31) WE NEED TO SELL OUR HOME FIRST.

32) MY SPOUSE NEEDS TO SEE IT FIRST.

33) MY UNCLE NEEDS TO SEE IT FIRST.

34) MY ATTORNEY NEEDS TO REVIEW THE CONTRACT (PAPERWORK) FIRST.

35) WE NEED TO THINK IT OVER.

36) WE WANT TO BUILD THIS CUSTOM HOME ON OUR OWN LAND BUT WE DON'T HAVE OUR LAND YET.

WE COULD GET THIS UP TO WAY OVER 100 OBJECTIONS BUT YOU GET THE POINT. ADD SOME TO IT.

> **"ACTUALLY ALL OBJECTIONS CAN BE BROKEN DOWN TO "THE ONLY SEVEN OBJECTIONS IN SELLING NEW HOMES™.""**
>
> — CHARLES CLARKE III

1) NOT READY.

2) NOT WILLING.

3) NOT ABLE.

4) NEED TO SELL OUR HOME FIRST.
   a) (ACTUALLY THIS IS UNDER THE CATEGORY OF "WE NEED TO TAKE CARE OF SOMETHING FIRST.)"
   b) NEEDING TO FIND A LOT (LAND) IS ALSO IN THIS CATEGORY FOR ON YOUR LOT BUILDERS.

5) YOUR PRICE IS TOO HIGH. THIS IS DIFFERENT THAN #3 WHICH IS "NOT ABLE" (CAN'T AFFORD IT).

6) NEED TO THINK IT OVER.

7) SOMEONE ELSE NEEDS TO SEE IT FIRST. (SPOUSE OR SOMEONE ELSE.) (COULD BE "MY ATTORNEY NEEDS TO READ THE CONTRACT FIRST)

IF SELLING ON THEIR LAND, AN 8TH OBJECTION COULD BE "WE DON'T HAVE LAND," BUT THAT IS REALLY OBJECTION #4 "WE NEED TO TAKE CARE OF SOMETHING ELSE FIRST."

OBJECTION #1 "NOT READY"

A READY BUYER IS SOMEONE WHO SAYS THEY "HAVE DECIDED TO MOVE" OR THAT THEY ARE "THINKING ABOUT MOVING."

A NOT READY BUYER IS SOMEONE WHO HAS "NOT DECIDED TO MOVE" OR WHO IS "NOT THINKING OF MOVING."

IT'S VERY IMPORTANT TO USE A WORKABLE, OPERATIONAL DEFINITION.

OBJECTION #2 "NOT WILLING"

A WILLING BUYER IS ALL ABOUT "PRODUCT;" THEY LIKE YOUR HOME AND COMMUNITY.

A "NOT WILLING" BUYER IS "SOMEONE WHO DOESN'T LIKE YOUR PRODUCT, YOUR HOUSE, OR COMMUNITY" (DOESN'T WORK FOR THEM.)

IF THEY DON'T LIKE YOU, YOU ARE AN EXTENSION OF THE PRODUCT. IF THEY DON'T LIKE YOUR SCHOOL DISTRICT OR ANYTHING ABOUT YOUR HOME, THAT IS PRODUCT.

OBJECTION #3: "NOT ABLE"

"NOT IN YOUR PRICE RANGE, DON'T HAVE THE DOWN PAYMENT, MONTHLY PAYMENT OR CREDIT."

WOULD YOU ASK SOMEONE (WHO TOLD YOU THEY HAVE A 450 CREDIT SCORE), "WHAT DO YOU THINK ABOUT GOING AHEAD WITH THIS TODAY?"

IF YOU SIGNED THAT COMMITMENT EARLIER, YOU SHOULD.

YOU NEVER KNOW WHEN THEY MIGHT HAVE A CO-SIGNER OR "MONEY BURIED IN THEIR BACKYARD."

BY ASKING THEM IT DOESN'T MEAN YOU HAVE TO WRITE IT UP. YOU ARE JUST FINDING OUT THEIR "INTENTIONS," SO YOU COULD POSSIBLY DO "CREDIT REPAIR" LATER.

OBJECTION #4 "NEED TO SELL OUR HOME"

A GOOD "MIND-SET" IS APPROXIMATELY 50% OF ALL PEOPLE THAT SAY THEY NEED TO SELL THEIR HOME, REALLY DON'T.

OBJECTION #5 "YOUR PRICE IS TOO HIGH"

THE LIE/MYTH THAT COVERED NEGOTIATING, LIE/MYTH #19 GOT INTO THIS.

OBJECTION #6 "WE NEED TO THINK IT OVER"

(A REAL OBJECTION, NOT A SMOKE SCREEN.) WRITE IT UP "SUBJECT TO THINKING IT OVER WITHIN 24 HOURS."

OBJECTION #7 "MY SPOUSE (OR SOMEONE ELSE) NEEDS TO APPROVE IT FIRST."

WRITE IT UP "SUBJECT TO (SOMEONE'S) APPROVAL WITHIN 24 HOURS."

ASSIGNMENT: ONCE A PERSON HAS LEFT AND THEY DIDN'T BUY FROM YOU, WRITE DOWN WHICH OBJECTION IT WAS. (WHY THEY DIDN'T BUY.)

CHALLENGE TO YOU: TRY TO COME UP WITH AN OBJECTION THAT DOES NOT FIT INTO ONE OF THESE CATEGORIES. YOU WON'T BE ABLE TO.

THINGS I AGREE WITH

THINGS I DISAGREE WITH

THINGS I NEED TO WORK ON

ACTION PLAN FOR ME

CHAPTER XXX

> **QUESTION #27:** SELLING HIGH END HOMES REQUIRES A VERY DIFFERENT SKILL SET FROM SELLING ENTRY LEVEL HOMES. YES/NO

LIE/MYTH #27: SELLING HIGH END HOMES IS DIFFERENT FROM SELLING LOWER PRICED HOMES

ANSWER: REALLY?

YOU'VE GOT THE POINT BY NOW.

IN MY SEMINARS AND CONSULTING, THIS QUESTION ALWAYS COMES UP IN SOME FORM OR ANOTHER. "ISN'T IT MORE DIFFICULT TO SELL HIGH-END HOMES?" OR THE REVERSE OF THAT IS, "ISN'T IT MORE DIFFICULT TO SELL "ENTRY" LEVEL HOMES?" MY ANSWER IS IT IS THE SAME SKILL SET, AND MY **BOLT™** PERSONALITIES COME INTO PLAY IN THE SAME WAY.

THE "BLOCK" IS OFTEN IN THE MIND OF THE SALESPERSON WHEN THEY ARE SHIFTED FROM ONE PRODUCT OR PRICE POINT TO THE NEXT. THE SAME PERCENTAGE OF BUYERS BUYING THE FIRST DAY (APPROXIMATELY 33%) REMAINS THE SAME. THE OBJECTION IS NOT WITH THE PRODUCT, BUT WITH THE SALESPERSON.

THIS NEXT STATEMENT COULD ACTUALLY BE A MYTH OF ITS OWN AND THAT IS "OUR CITY OR OUR STATE, OR OUR AREA IS DIFFERENT FROM ANYWHERE ELSE." MY ANSWER TO THAT IS **NOT REALLY!**

EVERYWHERE I GO, I GET THIS STATEMENT: "CHARLES YOUR PRINCIPLES ARE SOLID EVERYWHERE ELSE, BUT IT'S DIFFERENT HERE." AGAIN, IF YOU REALLY BELIEVE THAT, IT WILL ONLY INTERFERE WITH YOUR SELLING.

> **THE SELLING PROCESS IS NOT GENDER BASED, CITY BASED, PRODUCT BASED OR PRICE BASED. SELLING IS SELLING! THE PRODUCT IS DIFFERENT BUT THE SELLING PROCESS REMAINS THE SAME.**

NOTES

THINGS I AGREE WITH

THINGS I DISAGREE WITH

THINGS I NEED TO WORK ON

ACTION PLAN FOR ME

CHAPTER XXXI

> **QUESTION #28:** IT IS BEST TO ALWAYS ASK QUALIFYING QUESTIONS (READY, WILLING & ABLE), STANDING UP OVER THE COMMUNITY MAP WHERE THE BUYER IS RELAXED, RATHER THAN GOING INTO YOUR OFFICE IN THE FIRST COUPLE OF MINUTES. YES/NO

> # LIE/MYTH #28: IT IS BETTER TO ASK QUALIFYING QUESTIONS STANDING UP, RATHER THAN ASKING THEM TO COME INTO YOUR OFFICE AND SIT DOWN (FOR THE FIRST COUPLE MINUTES).

THIS MYTH IS QUITE HUGE, BECAUSE I REALLY BELIEVE OUR INDUSTRY HAS BEEN DOING THIS "THING" OF QUALIFYING (SO IMPORTANT) VERY WRONG FOR DECADES. IT HAS JUST KEPT PERPETUATING FROM ONE DECADE TO THE NEXT.

WE ALL KNOW THERE IS THE CRITICAL PATH OF SELLING AND AS DISCUSSED, IT HAS BEEN IN EXISTENCE FOR WELL OVER 100 YEARS. OUR INDUSTRY REALLY DOES NOT FOLLOW IT.

> **SCENARIO #1 – (BAD VERSION) – NOT HOW TO DO IT**

SALESPERSON WELCOMES THE PROSPECTIVE BUYER AND SAYS SOMETHING LIKE, "IS THIS YOUR FIRST TIME IN?"

PROSPECTIVE BUYER SAYS, "YES."

THEN THE SALESPERSON POSITIONS HIMSELF OR HERSELF AROUND THE COMMUNITY MAP AND STARTS TALKING.

"SINCE THIS IS YOUR FIRST TIME HERE, LET ME TELL YOU A LITTLE ABOUT THE COMMUNITY. THEN I'LL TELL YOU ABOUT THE BUILDER, AND THEN THE FLOOR PLANS THAT ARE HUNG ON THE WALL. THEN WE CAN GO INTO THE MODEL AND I'LL EXPLAIN OUR CONSTRUCTION."

HOW MANY OF YOU KNOW THAT THAT PARTICULAR PRESENTATION IS GOING ON IN YOUR CITY TODAY? NOT WITH YOU, BUT WITH OTHER BUILDERS.

MAYBE YOU DON'T DO IT THAT WAY, BUT THAT IS WHAT IS BEING DONE AND EVEN BEING TAUGHT TO DO, IN MANY COMPANIES.

LET'S LOOK AT THAT FROM STRICTLY A CRITICAL PATH PRESENTATION.

CRITICAL PATH AGAIN

1) MEET, GREET AND CONNECT WITH THEM

2) QUALIFY FOR
   A) READY
   B) WILLING
   C) ABLE

3) DEMONSTRATE

4) SELECTION

5) OVERCOME OBJECTIONS AND CLOSE THE SALE

ANALYZE WHAT TOOK PLACE IN THE SITUATION I JUST LAID OUT.

THEY DID A MEETING AND GREETING, NO CONNECTION, AND THEN WENT RIGHT INTO DEMONSTRATING WITHOUT ANY QUALIFYING.

SCENARIO #2 – (BAD VERSION) – NOT HOW TO DO IT

"HELLO! I AM AND YOU ARE? WHAT BRINGS YOU OUT LOOKING AT OUR NEW HOMES TODAY?"

ANSWER, "WE'RE JUST LOOKING."

"WHAT ARE YOU LOOKING FOR?"

"I'M NOT SURE."

"ARE YOU LOOKING FOR A 1 OR 2 STORY HOME? WHAT TYPE OF HOME ARE YOU LOOKING FOR? LET ME TELL YOU ABOUT OUR HOMES."

NO MEETING AND GREETING, NOT REALLY ANY QUALIFYING; JUST RIGHT INTO DEMONSTRATION.

SCENARIO #3 – (BAD VERSION) – REALLY NOT HOW TO DO IT

"WELCOME. IS THIS YOUR FIRST TIME HERE? (IF YES) THEN WHY DON'T YOU LOOK THORUGH OUR MODEL AND THEN I'LL ANSWER ANY OF YOUR QUESTIONS."

AND IT GOES ON FROM THERE.

LOOK AT WHAT IS MISSING. NO CONNECTION AND NO QUALIFYING FOR READY. JUST JUMPING RIGHT INTO "SELF DEMONSTRATION", WITHOUT EVEN KNOWING REALLY WHY THEY ARE THERE OR IF THEY ARE REALLY THINKING ABOUT MOVING OR HAVE THEY DECIDED TO MOVE.

RE-THINK ABOUT DOING IT THE FOLLOWING WAY. (IT WORKS!)

FROM CHARLES J. CLARKE III, "THE ART OF ASKING QUESTIONS™"

BOX #1: QUALIFYING FOR READY

WHEN THEY FIRST COME IN:

    i. "WHAT BRINGS YOU OUT LOOKING AT OUR NEW HOMES TODAY?" WAIT FOR AN ANSWER.
    1. "COME ON INTO MY OFFICE AND LET ME FIND OUT MORE ABOUT YOUR NEEDS IN A HOME."

IN THE OFFICE CONNECT WITH THEM:

    2. "HOW LONG HAVE YOU BEEN LOOKING FOR A NEW HOME?"
    3. "WHAT IS YOUR SITUATION, ARE YOU NEW TO THE AREA?"
    4. "WHERE DO YOU CURRENTLY LIVE?"
    5. "HOW LONG HAVE YOU LIVED THERE?"
    6. "DO YOU NEED TO SELL YOUR HOME? IF SO, IS IT ON THE MARKET?"

8. "ARE YOU THINKING ABOUT MOVING OR HAVE YOU ALREADY DECIDED TO MOVE?

9. "WHEN WOULD YOU LIKE TO BE IN YOUR NEW HOME?"

YOU CAN GET 90% TO COME INTO YOUR OFFICE. IT WORKS BETTER THAN QUALIFYING STANDING UP.

I'M NOT SUGGESTING YOU DO THESE QUESTIONS VERBATIM, BUT JUST HAVE THE GENERAL FLOW.

BULLS <u>WILL</u> COME INTO YOUR OFFICE IF YOU SAY SOMETHING LIKE, "COME ON INTO MY OFFICE AND LET ME QUICKLY FIND OUT MORE ABOUT YOUR NEEDS IN A HOME, SO I DON'T TALK ABOUT A LOT OF 'STUFF' ABOUT WHICH YOU HAVE NO INTEREST, AND THEN I'LL SHOW YOU OUR HOMES." **REMEMBER BULLS DON'T GO OUT TO SHOP; THEY GO OUT TO BUY.**

BOX #2: QUALIFYING FOR WILLING

DURING THIS TIME, START FILLING OUT THE REGISTRATION FORM YOURSELF. (NOT ASKING THEM TO FILL IT OUT – YOU GET MORE ACCURACY THIS WAY.)

1. "WHAT ARE YOUR NEEDS IN A HOME, SUCH AS THE NUMBER OF BEDROOMS, BATHROOMS, POSSIBLE SQUARE FOOTAGE, OR ANYTHING ELSE THAT CAN HELP ME HELP YOU?"
2. "HAVE YOU BEEN TO OUR WEBSITE?"
3. "WHICH PLAN DID YOU LIKE THE BEST FOR YOUR NEEDS?"

BOX #3: QUALIFYING FOR ABLE

1. "OUR HOMES ARE IN THE PRICE RANGE OF $_____ TO OVER $_____.
2. "WHAT PRICE RANGE DID YOU HAVE IN MIND?"
3. "WOULD YOU BE PAYING CASH OR WOULD YOU BE USING A MORTGAGE?
4. "HAVE YOU BEEN PRE-QUALIFIED BY A MORTGAGE COMPANY?"

BOX #4: HOW WOULD YOU LIKE TO PROCEED?

HOW WOULD YOU LIKE TO PROCEED?

WE COULD NEXT

- A) GO SEE THE HOME THAT IS UNDER CONSTRUCTION, OF THE FLOOR PLAN YOU SAW ONLINE.
- B) SEE THE MODEL.
- C) HAVE ME EXPLAIN SOME OF OUR OTHER FLOOR PLANS.
- D) ANSWER SOME OF YOUR QUESTIONS.
- E) TELL YOU ABOUT OUR BUILDER AND OUR BUILDER'S STORY.

"HOW WOULD YOU LIKE TO PROCEED?"

THESE FIRST FOUR BOXES ARE THE "BEGINNING" OF THE GAME OF SELLING

WHAT PERCENTAGE OF ALL YOUR POTENTIAL BUYERS DO YOU THINK WILL COME IN TO YOUR OFFICE? I USUALLY GET GUESSES OF ABOUT 50%. YOU WILL GET 90%+ OF ALL YOUR POTENTIAL BUYERS TO COME INTO YOUR OFFICE FOR REAL QUALIFYING NOT JUST QUALIFYING WHILE THEY ARE BEING DISTRACTED BY YOU, TRYING TO DEMONSTRATE AT THE SAME TIME.

ALL OWLS AND LAMBS WILL COME IN.

WILL BULLS COME IN? CERTAINLY.

MODIFIED FOR THE BULL: "COME ON INTO MY OFFICE. (IF YOU DON'T HAVE AN OFFICE, COME OVER HERE AND SIT DOWN.) LET ME FIND OUT A LITTLE MORE ABOUT YOUR NEEDS IN A HOME,

SO I DON'T WASTE YOUR TIME TALKING ABOUT A BUNCH OF STUFF IN WHICH YOU HAVE NO INTEREST."

IN THIS SYSTEM, FOR THE FIRST 3 MINUTES (APPROXIMATELY) YOU ARE NOT SELLING AT ALL. YOU ARE NOT TELLING ABOUT THE BUILDER, UNLESS THEY ASK. YOU ARE DEVOTING ALL YOUR ATTENTION TO THEM, FINDING OUT THEIR READY, WILLING & ABLE NEEDS.

IT'S NOT UNTIL A FEW MINUTES LATER THAT YOU ACTUALLY DO

> **#5: DEMONSTRATION – THE "MIDDLE" OF THE GAME OF SELLING**

> **TELLING AND SHOWING ALL ABOUT YOUR PRODUCT AND ANSWERING THEIR QUESTIONS ABOUT YOUR COMPANY, YOUR COMMUNITY, HOMES, HOME SITES, SCHOOLS, ETC.**

3 PARTS OF THE "GAME OF SELLING"

1) **BEGINNING**
2) **MIDDLE**
3) **END**

BEGINNING – QUALIFYING FOR READY, WILLING AND ABLE (BOXES 1 – 4) WITH <u>YOU</u> FILLING OUT THE REGISTRATION CARD AND ASKING HOW <u>THEY</u> WANT TO PROCEED.

MIDDLE – DEMONSTRATION (BOX 5)

END – OVERCOMING OBJECTIONS AND CLOSING THE SALE (BOXES 6 – 8)

PRACTICE, DRILL AND REHEARSE METHODICALLY UNTIL IT BECOMES NATURAL FOR YOU.

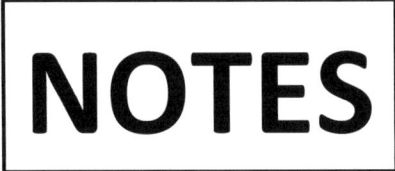

THINGS I AGREE WITH

THINGS I DISAGREE WITH

THINGS I NEED TO WORK ON

ACTION PLAN FOR ME

CHAPTER XXXII

QUESTION #29: EVEN IF THE BUYER IS A READY, WILLING AND ABLE BUYER AND SAYS, "NO, THEY DO NOT WANT TO GO AHEAD WITH THIS TODAY," IT WOULD BE RUDE AND PUSHY TO BRING OUT THE PURCHASE AGREEMENT AND START WRITING ON IT. YES/NO

LIE/MYTH #29: EVEN IF THE BUYER IS READY, WILLING AND ABLE AND SAYS, "NO, THEY DO NOT WANT TO GO AHEAD WITH THIS TODAY," IT WOULD BE RUDE AND PUSHY TO BRING OUT THE PURCHASE AGREEMENT AND START WRITING.

SEE WHAT YOU THINK OF THE <u>FLOW</u> OF THIS.

REMEMBER, THIS IS WITH A

3 GREEN DOT BUYER

3 GREEN DOTS: READY, WILLING AND ABLE BUYER

THEY SAID THEY HAD 1) DECIDED TO MOVE, 2) THEY LIKED YOUR COMMUNITY, HOME, AND HOME SITE, AND 3) THEY CAN AFFORD IT, BUT WHEN YOU SAID "WHAT DO YOU THINK ABOUT GOING AHEAD WITH THIS TODAY?" THEY SAID "NO," <u>AFTER</u> YOU ASKED THEM THE "FIVE MAGIC QUESTIONS™."

BOX #6: FIVE MAGIC QUESTIONS™:

At the home they've chosen (the model, a furnished home, a home under construction, or the home site):

You Ask: The Five Magic Questions™:

- How do you like this community?
- Is it a community you would like to live in?
- Which of our homes do you like best for your needs?
- Is this a home you would like to own?
- **"What Do You Think About Going Ahead With This Today™?"**

BOX #7: COME BACK TO MY OFFICE

If the answer is yes, go back to your office and write it up. **IF THE ANSWER IS NO**

- **YOU ASK WHY TO FLUSH OUT THE OBJECTION.**
- **COME ON BACK TO MY OFFICE AND LET ME GIVE YOU SOME ADDITIONAL INFORMATION FOR YOU TO TAKE HOME WITH YOU!**
- **AND AT THAT TIME, I WILL SHOW YOU OUR "PURCHASE AGREEMENT" FOR IF AND WHEN YOU EVER PURCHASE HERE, YOU Will KNOW WHAT IT LOOKS LIKE.**

BOX #8: CONTRACT "Second Chance Close™"

Back at the office where they have already been:

AS I HAVE MENTIONED: THIS IS OUR PURCHASE AGREEMENT THAT I SAID I WAS GOING TO SHOW YOU! Let me just fill in a few lines so you can take it home and know what it looks like.

1. This is the address of that property. (Start with the address.)
2. This is the price of the home that you liked.
3. This is the earnest money (deposit.)

At the bottom of the purchase agreement, I wrote "Subject to: (Their Objection)"

- Subject to spouse approval within 24 hours.
- Subject to thinking it over within 24 hours.
- Subject to whatever their objection was.

You're not being pushy; you are just giving them a SECOND chance to say "Yes" with a "Subject To."

You can have any combination of these. You always have to have an ending date! If they don't want to sign it, you still give them a copy of it and you have increased the probability they will come back. Before they leave you put their names at the top.

AGAIN, EVEN IF THEY DO NOT SIGN YOU HAVE INCREASED THE "PROBABILITY" THAT THEY WILL COME BACK BECAUSE YOU HAVE PERSONALIZED THE PURCHASE AGREEMENT WITH THEIR NAME AND THEIR ADDRESS OF THE PROPERTY THEY CHOSE. OF COURSE, THERE IS A LOT MORE DETAIL TO BE EXPLAINED ABOUT THIS, BUT THE POINT IS START WRITING IT UP WITH 3 GREEN DOT BUYERS.

USE THE PURCHASE AGREEMENT AS A TOOL.

"STRETCH THE RUBBER BAND, BUT DON'T BREAK IT."

THIS "SECOND CHANCE CLOSE" IS OBVIOUSLY **NOT FOOL PROOF,** BUT DO YOU THINK IT WOULD INCREASE THE PROBABILITY OF THEM ACTUALLY SIGNING?

AFTER THEY HAVE SAID "NO," WHILE BACK AT THE PROPERTY, MANY SALESPEOPLE MAKE THE MISTAKE OF SAYING: "THIS IS WHAT WE COULD DO. WE COULD WRITE THIS UP SUBJECT TO YOUR SPOUSE'S APPROVAL."

THE DIFFERENCE BETWEEN THAT AND WHAT I AM SUGGESTING IS, YOU SAY:

BACK AT THE OFFICE

OVER THE CONTRACT

"THIS IS WHAT I HAVE DONE."

WHICH HAS THE HIGHER PROBABILITY OF GOING THROUGH?

AN EXAMPLE WOULD BE YOU ARE AT A RESTAURANT AND THE WAITER ASKS IF YOU CARE FOR A DESSERT.

I COULD BRING OUT THE DESSERT TRAY VERSUS

"THIS IS WHAT I HAVE DONE"

"HERE IS THE DESSERT TRAY"

THEN EXPLAINING THE DESSERT TRAY.

WE DO NOT USE THE PURCHASE AGREEMENT ENOUGH AS A CLOSING TOOL. START WRITING! CHARLES J. CLARKE III

WHICH IS MORE POWERFUL?

WHEN SOME SALESPEOPLE FIRST HEAR THIS SECOND CHANCE CLOSE, THEY THINK IT IS <u>TOO PUSHY</u>.

YOUR THOUGHTS?

IT'S ALL IN THE PRESENTATION!

REVIEW OF MY 8 BOXES

BOX #1: QUALIFY FOR <u>READY</u> (WHILE SITTING DOWN)

BOX #2: QUALIFY FOR <u>WILLING</u> (WHILE SITTING DOWN)

(START FILLING OUT REGISTRATION CARD)

BOX #3: QUALIFY FOR <u>ABLE</u> (WHILE SITTING DOWN)

BOX #4: "HOW WOULD YOU LIKE TO PROCEED?"

GIVING THEM CHOICES

THESE FIRST 4 BOXES ARE THE <u>BEGINNING OF THE GAME OF SELLING</u> AND ARE DONE <u>IN YOUR OFFICE</u> (3 TO 5 MINUTES) – (WITH BULLS 2 MINUTES)

THE MIDDLE OF THE GAME OF SELLING IS

BOX #5: DEMONSTRATION (ALL ABOUT YOUR COMPANY AND YOUR HOMES)

PROCEEDING THE WAY <u>THEY</u> WANT TO PROCEED

BOX #6: THE FIVE MAGIC QUESTIONS WITH <u>ALL,</u> EVEN 3 RED DOT BUYERS (NOT READY, NOT WILLING, NOT ABLE)

BOX #7: BACK TO YOUR OFFICE EITHER TO WRITE IT UP OR TO GO OVER THE CONTRACT

BOX #8: SECOND CHANCE CLOSE™ (THIS ACTUALLY IS WHEN CLOSING REALLY BEGINS.)

BOX 8 IS WHERE YOU WOULD REALLY USE YOUR SKILL SET WITH "KILLER CLOSES FOR DIFFERENT PERSONALITIES™" WITH 3 GREEN DOT BUYERS.

REMEMBER A 3 GREEN DOT BUYER IS READY, WILLING AND ABLE <u>EVEN</u> IF THEY HAVE AN OBJECTION: WE NEED TO SELL OUR HOME, SPOUSE IS NOT HERE, MY ATTORNEY NEEDS TO SEE THE CONTRACT FIRST, WE DON'T HAVE OUR LAND (OR ON YOUR LOT BUYERS IF A CUSTOM HOME), WE NEED TO THINK IT OVER, WE HAVEN'T DECIDED WHICH OF YOUR HOMES IS BEST FOR US, WE DON'T KNOW WHAT AMENITIES TO CHOOSE, WE HAVE MORE QUESTIONS, ETC.

☆☆☆ ASKING A POTENTIAL BUYER, "<u>WHAT DO YOU THINK ABOUT GOING AHEAD WITH THIS TODAY</u>™?" IS <u>ONLY THE "BEGINNING"</u>. IT'S ONLY A "TRIAL CLOSE" LIKE "HOW DO YOU LIKE THESE CABINETS?" IF YOU THINK OF IT LIKE THAT, YOU CAN DO IT WITH EVERYONE, EVEN RED DOTS.

"REAL CLOSING" IS UNDER BOX #8 WITH 3 GREEN DOT BUYERS WHO ARE STILL SAYING "NO." THIS IS THE BIG CHALLENGE OF A MASTER CLOSER.

READ THIS CHAPTER AGAIN RIGHT NOW.

YOUR THOUGHTS?

NOTES

THINGS I AGREE WITH

THINGS I DISAGREE WITH

THINGS I NEED TO WORK ON

ACTION PLAN FOR ME

CHAPTER XXXIII

> **QUESTION #30:** MASTER CLOSERS CAN NOT OVERCOME BAD OR FLAWED DESIGN AND PRODUCT. YES/NO

LIE/MYTH #30: MASTER CLOSERS CAN NOT OVERCOME BAD OR FLAWED DESIGN

BE CAREFUL WITH THIS ONE! NOT EVERYONE LIKES OR DISLIKES WHAT YOU LIKE OR DISLIKE. WHAT **YOU** THINK IS BAD DESIGN OR FLAWED PRODUCT, SOMEONE ELSE MAY NOT THINK THE SAME WAY. THEY MAY LOVE IT!

EXAMPLE: IN PHOENIX, A COMMUNITY <u>HAD NOT HAD A SALE FOR 90 DAYS</u>. THE SALES LADY HAD "ISSUES" WITH THE MODEL, FLOOR PLANS, INVENTORY HOMES, LAYOUT OF THE COMMUNITY AND ITS PRICING. SHE HAD BEEN WITH THAT COMPANY FOR SEVERAL YEARS AND HAD RECENTLY BEEN TRANSFERRED TO THIS COMMUNITY WITH ZERO LOT LINES. SHE SAID THE COMMUNITY WAS BASICALLY <u>BAD PRODUCT</u> AND THE FLOOR PLANS WERE <u>FLAWED DESIGNS</u>.

I SUGGESTED WE TRANSFER HER FROM THAT COMMUNITY AND HIRE A BRAND NEW SALESPERSON FOR THAT COMMUNITY. WE HELD A "GROUP INTERVIEW" AND HIRED A MAN; JERRY M. WHO HAD NEVER PROFESSIONALLY SOLD ANYTHING IN HIS LIFE. HE WAS IMMEDIATELY PUT THROUGH MY MASTER CLOSER TRILOGY PLUS TWO ADDITIONAL DAYS OF ROLE PLAYING AND PDR (PRACTICE, DRILL AND REHEARSING.)

<u>**HERE'S THE BOTTOM LINE:**</u>

IN HIS FIRST 30 DAYS OF SELLING, HE HAD 14 "GROSS" SALES AND 12 "NET" SALES: FULL PRICE, NO "GIVEAWAYS," NO CHANGE ORDERS AND 12 VERY HAPPY HOME OWNERS. WHEN THE PREVIOUS SALESLADY WAS SELLING, THE OBJECTIONS WERE **HER OWN**. DON'T LET THAT INTERFERE WITH YOU. JERRY M. HAD NO PREVIOUS INTERNAL OBJECTIONS OR "MYTHS IN SELLING NEW HOMES™. HE FOLLOWED THE MASTER CLOSER PROGRAM. **WHAT ABOUT YOU?**

THINGS I AGREE WITH

THINGS I DISAGREE WITH

THINGS I NEED TO WORK ON

ACTION PLAN FOR ME

CHAPTER XXXIV

CONCLUSION

WHAT ARE YOUR THOUGHTS?

> HAS THIS BOOK HELPED YOU TO THINK DIFFERENTLY ABOUT THE SALES PROCESS?

THIS IS A TYPE OF BOOK THAT YOU REALLY NEED TO READ SEVERAL TIMES MORE. DO YOU THINK ANY DIFFERENTLY ABOUT THE SALES PROCESS THAN YOU DID BEFORE READING THIS?

> WOULD YOU AGREE THAT THIS IS NOT AN "ORDINARY" BOOK?

GO BACK AND LOOK AT THE LIES/MYTHS AGAIN IN THE VERY BEGINNING OF THE BOOK. HAVE YOUR OPINIONS CHANGED? HOW MANY YES'S DO YOU NOW HAVE?

MAKE A LIST OF THINGS YOU ARE GOING TO BE DOING DIFFERENTLY.

IF YOUR CLOSING RATIO IS EXCELLENT AT A 1 IN 10, IS THERE SOMETHING YOU COULD SAY OR DO TO GET JUST 1 OF THOSE 9 THAT GOT AWAY, TO PURCHASE? (YOU KNOW THE DRILL.)

ARE THERE ANY PRINCIPLES IN THIS BOOK THAT WILL HELP YOU DO THAT? WHICH ONES? IF YOU JUST GET 1 OF THOSE 9 THAT GOT AWAY, YOU WOULD BE A 2 IN 10 OR A 1 IN 5 AND YOU WOULD:

> **BECOME A MASTER CLOSER**
>
> AND DRASTICALLY INCREASE YOUR INCOME AND THE PROFIT OF YOUR BUILDER.

> **QUESTION EVERYTHING!**
>
> <u>QUESTION STATEMENTS AND PREMISES IN THIS BOOK AND IN OTHER BOOKS</u> AND THUS BECOME A STRONGER AND BETTER SALESPERSON, SERVING OUR INDUSTRY AND MOST IMPORTANTLY THE CUSTOMER.

IF YOU DON'T AGREE WITH SOME OF THE PRINCIPLES IN THIS BOOK, THEN DON'T USE THEM.

> USE WHAT IS COMFORTABLE FOR YOU.

I WOULD LOVE TO BE KEPT IN YOUR LOOP.

PLEASE LET ME HEAR FROM YOU. I MEAN THAT!

EMAIL ME YOUR THOUGHTS ABOUT THIS BOOK. LET'S HAVE A DIALOGUE.

SEND US YOUR "SUCCESS STORIES" TO BE INCLUDED IN MY NEXT BOOK.

INVITE ME INTO YOUR COMPANY FOR PERSONAL SEMINARS AND CONSULTING.

THANK YOU.

CHARLES J. CLARKE III, MIRM

CELL: 678-516-4833

EMAIL: CHARLES@PERSONALITYSELLING.COM

IF YOU REALLY LIKED THIS BOOK, ORDER A COPY FOR <u>EVERYONE</u> IN YOUR COMPANY; CONSTRUCTION, OPERATIONS, SALES AND MARKETING!

MAKE THESE PRINCIPLES A WAY OF LIFE IN YOUR COMPANY!

CHAPTER XXXV

SUMMARY OF "LIES AND MYTHS WE HAVE BEEN TAUGHT IN: SELLING NEW HOMES™"

#1) A SALESPERSON HAS TO ALWAYS EARN THE RIGHT TO CLOSE.

#2) IT IS OF UTMOST IMPORTANCE TO TALK ABOUT SOCIAL FIRST (BUILD RAPPORT) RATHER THAN BUSINESS (COMMERCE) FIRST.

#3) IN NEW HOME SALES IT IS OF UTMOST IMPORTANCE TO SELL THE CONCEPT OF THE "BUILDER'S VISION" AND TELL THE BUILDER'S STORY AT THE BEGINNING, IN THE FIRST FEW MINUTES.

#4) OF ALL THE STEPS OF THE CRITICAL PATH OF SELLING NEW HOMES, THE OUTRIGHT MOST IMPORTANT STEP IS "DEMONSTRATION," IN ORDER TO DIFFERENTIATE THE BUILDER AND THE NEW HOME FROM EXISTING (USED) HOMES AND OTHER COMPETITORS.

#5) IT WOULD BE TOO PUSHY TO 100% OF THE TIME, TO ASK FOR THE SALE.

#6) IT IS "VERY RARE" FOR SOMEONE TO "BUY" (GIVE A CHECK AND SIGN A CONTRACT), THE FIRST TIME THEY SEE THE COMMUNITY OR HOME IN PERSON.

#7) IF A PERSON IS MARRIED THEY WOULD NOT "BUY" IF THEIR SPOUSE IS NOT THERE.

#8) CROSSED ARMS AND NO SMILE MEANS THAT A PERSON IS DEFENSIVE.

#9) IT IS VERY IMPORTANT THAT THE SALESPERSON TAKES CONTROL AND MAINTAINS CONTROL THROUGHOUT THE SALES PROCESS, AND THAT THE BUYER IS TOTALLY MADE AWARE OF THIS.

#10) IT IS VERY IMPORTANT TO STATE, RESTATE AND VERIFY WHAT THE BUYER JUST SAID.

#11) IF A BUYER ASKS FOR THE PRICE RIGHT AWAY, THE SALESPERSON SHOULD AVOID TELLING THE BUYER THE PRICE RIGHT AWAY AND STAY ON COURSE.

#12) IF A COUPLE IS MARRIED, THE WOMAN ALWAYS MAKES THE FINAL DECISION IN BUYING.

#13) EVEN IF THERE IS NOT AN URGENT SITUATION, THEN THE SALESPERSON NEEDS TO CREATE "URGENCY," IN ORDER TO MOTIVATE THE BUYER.

#14) MEN ARE ALWAYS MORE "LOGICAL" IN BUYING A NEW HOME, WHILE WOMEN ARE ALWAYS MORE "EMOTIONAL."

#15) THE KITCHEN AND THE MASTER BATHROOM, WERE AND ARE STILL, THE MOST IMPORTANT ROOMS IN THE NEW HOME FOR A BUYER.

#16) IT IS OF UTMOST IMPORTANCE TO FIND "COMMON GROUND" WITH THE BUYER AND MAINTAIN THAT COMMON GROUND THROUGHOUT THE PROCESS.

#17) MEMORIZING "SCRIPTS," "WORD FOR WORD," AND USING THESE MEMORIZED SCRIPTS IS EXTREMELY IMPORTANT FOR THE SALESPERSON TO BECOME THE ABSOLUTE BEST.

#18) A "1 IN 10" CLOSING RATIO (10%) IS THE ULTIMATE CLOSING RATIO FOR WHICH A SALESPERSON SHOULD STRIVE.

#19) IT IS BEST TO ALWAYS HAVE THE PRICE OF THE HOME HIGHER THAN WHAT THE BUILDER WOULD SELL IT, SO YOU CAN NEGOTIATE THE PRICE LOWER.

#20) THE MOST IMPORTANT ACCOMPLISHMENT A NEW HOME SALES CONSULTANT CAN ACCOMPLISH ON THE FIRST VISIT IS TO GIVE THE BEST PRESENTATION POSSIBLE TO GET THE BUYER EXCITED ENOUGH TO COME BACK.

#21) 92% OF ALL POTENTIAL BUYERS HAVE ALREADY GONE TO YOUR WEBSITE BEFORE VISITING YOU.

#22) ALL BUYERS BUY WITH EMOTION AND JUSTIFY IT WITH LOGIC.

#23) IN SELLING TO ACTIVE ADULT BUYERS (50 YEARS+) THEY REALLY NEED TO BE TREATED DIFFERENTLY AND CERTAINLY WOULD NOT BUY THE FIRST DAY.

#24) SELLING RESORT COMMUNITIES IS VERY DIFFERENT FROM SELLING NON-RESORT COMMUNITIES.

#25) SELLING CUSTOM HOMES "ON THEIR LOT" IS VERY DIFFERENT, AND IF POTENTIAL BUYERS DON'T ALREADY HAVE THEIR OWN LOT (LAND) IN PLACE, THEY CERTAINLY WOULD NOT PURCHASE THE FIRST DAY.

#26) THERE COULD BE LITERALLY 100+ OBJECTIONS TO WHY THEY DON'T BUY ONE OF MY HOMES.

#27) SELLING HIGH END HOMES REQUIRES A VERY DIFFERENT SKILL SET FROM SELLING ENTRY LEVEL HOMES.

#28) IT IS BEST TO ALWAYS ASK QUALIFYING QUESTIONS (READY, WILLING & ABLE), STANDING UP OVER THE COMMUNITY MAP WHERE THE BUYER IS RELAXED, RATHER THAN GOING INTO YOUR OFFICE, IN THE FIRST COUPLE OF MINUTES.

#29) EVEN IF THE BUYER IS A READY, WILLING AND ABLE BUYER AND SAYS, "NO, THEY DO NOT WANT TO GO AHEAD WITH THIS TODAY," IT WOULD BE RUDE AND PUSHY TO BRING OUT THE PURCHASE AGREEMENT AND START WRITING ON IT.

#30) MASTER CLOSERS CAN NOT OVER COME BAD OR FLAWED DESIGN AND PRODUCT.

Bring Charles J. Clarke III personally into your company for his Three-Day Master Closer Trilogy or just one day, which could be "Lies and Myths We Have Been Taught in Selling New Homes™."

Description of Charles J. Clarke III's

Master Closer Trilogy

<u>Part I</u>-"Bulls, Owls, Lambs and Tigers®: Personality Selling™"

- Detailed Description and Examples
- 11 Ways to Identify Each Personality within the first two minutes
- Self-Testing
- "Closing for Different Personalities"
- 100% of the time asking, "What do you think about going ahead with this today?"
- The Only 7 Objections™
- "Negotiating Skills for Each Personality™"
- Becoming the Master Closer (1 in 5 Closing Ratio)
- "Closing, Closing, Closing"
- Much, Much More

<u>Part II</u>-An Entire Day of: "The Only 7 Objections with Specific Detailed Strategies of How to Overcome Each Objection Depending on Their Animal Personality™", Role Playing with each Objection and with each Personality. Also Role Playing with a couple being married to an opposite Personality.

Objections have a personality of their own.

(We usually overcome objections the way we would want them overcome for us and thus miss the target, half to three-quarters of the time.)

<u>Part III</u>- "The New Critical Path for Each Animal Personality™" *(We often have only one Critical Path that does not work with all four personalities! The Bull will not tolerate the traditional Owl Critical Path.)*

Part III also includes "Killer Closes for Different Personalities™". **(A detailed look at <u>46 different closes</u>, examining which closes work and don't work for each personality.)**

Example: Urgency Closes <u>only</u> work for Bulls and Tigers and Urgency Closes actually make Lambs and Owls <u>not</u> want to buy from you.

A special segment will be added on "Monster Goal Setting and Creating a Burning Desire for Success."

<u>**Attend a three-day selling conclave twice a year for selling new homes plus a two-day management retreat at the end, held in Orlando or Las Vegas**</u>**.** <u>**Sign up for the reasonably priced "Monthly Phone Coaching**</u>**."**

Please email <u>CJ@personalityselling.com</u> for pricing and details.

About The Author

Charles J. Clarke III-MIRM and past MIRM Instructor

(Master in Residential Marketing)

Charles J. Clarke III has one of those very unusual and varied backgrounds for being one of the Nation's TOP Consultants and one of the most sought after speakers to the Home Building and Real Estate Industry.

Among some of his accomplishments are:

- Undergraduate work at Miami University, Oxford, Ohio
- Castle and Cooke Graduate Scholarship to the University of Hawaii for his Master's Degree (M.A.) in Sociology with emphasis in Psychology
- Instructor at the University of Maryland and University of Arizona while working toward his Ph.D. in Sociology with an emphasis in Psychology
- Department Chairman and Professor of Sociology at Mt. Mercy College in Cedar Rapids, Iowa
- President of "Clarke Property Management"/"Clarke Investments Inc."/"Charles Clarke Consulting Inc."
- 1st Vice President of Century 21's Regional Office of Texas and Louisiana
- National Training Director for Today's American Builder out of Houston, Texas
- President and Regional Director for Todays American Builder for the State of Florida
- Sales Manager for one of the Nation's Larger Builders in the United States, North Carolina Division
- Partner in "The Proview Group"-Video Sales Series for Sales Managers (Video Tape of the Month)
- Partner in PersonalityID.com
- 3 Separate Terms as Trustee for the National Sales and Marketing Council for NAHB
- Featured Speaker at National Home Builders Association since 1985 (Super Bowl Sales Rally)
- Featured Speaker for National Association of Realtors®
- National and International Sales and Marketing Expert. Chosen as one of the only Sales and Marketing Expert for the 1st Ever International Builder's show for NAHB, in Budapest, Hungry (Translated in 6 different Languages.)
- Has spoken to many HBA's & SMC's in the U.S. and Canada.
- Founder and Chairman of State of Florida's State SMC
- Founder or Co-Founder of several SMC's
- Consultant and Speaker to many of the Nation's Top Builders, Developers and Realtors®
- Author and International Speaker
- Creator of "Bulls, Owls, Lambs & Tigers®: Personality Selling™."
- Father of 4 Adult Children: Charles Joseph Clarke IV (CJ), Charles Joseph Clarke V (Joey), Tamara "Charles" Clarke, and Tiffany "Charles" Clarke Barrett

Made in the USA
San Bernardino, CA
11 November 2013